"Not giving up on ourselves or each other is increasingly crucial in a culture weathering hard things. I love the voices of (in)courage in this book, representing real-life issues and helping us find strength in our shared hope in Jesus."

Lisa Whittle, bestselling author, Bible teacher, and podcast host

"In the midst of a world that can often feel fractured and divided, *Come Sit with Me* is a welcome breath of fresh air. The stories of friendship across political divides and theological differences and despite difficulties touched me deeply. This book left me feeling so encouraged, and it infused me with practical suggestions and ideas on how to be a better friend to others. It is a much-needed message in this hurting, lonely world!"

Crystal Paine, *New York Times* bestselling author, podcaster, and founder of MoneySavingMom.com

"Our lives can often seem so disconnected. What I love about *Come Sit with Me* is it reminds us that God intends for our worlds to collide—both lovingly and distinctively. Our differences, our doubts, and our desires are actually designed to lead us individually and collectively into our destiny. A must-read for all who desire heaven on earth."

Marshawn Evans Daniels, Godfidence® coach, TV personality, reinvention strategist for women, and founder of SheProfits.com

"Encouraging, inspirational, and practical—these are the first three words that come to mind as I read *Come Sit with Me*. If ever there was a time we needed a book on loving through disagreements, living with discomfort, and delighting in our differences, it's now. This book is a friend as well as a gentle guide for those of us neck-deep in these struggles. Hearing the stories of others doesn't solve all our problems, but the wisdom of those who've been where we are helps. And the wisdom of those who point us back to Jesus at every twist and bend? Well, that is one way God redeems those heartbreak moments. We all struggle. I'm grateful for the storytellers who allow God to use their suffering to minister to others. I needed this book. My guess is you need it too."

Kris Camealy, author of *Everything Is Yours*
and founder of Refine {the retreat}

"*Come Sit with Me* is a beautifully written collection of stories covering relevant and challenging scenarios we face today. A wide range of women from different life stages, experiences, and ethnic backgrounds share from their personal lives in helpful and hope-filled ways. Honest, relatable, and practical, the pages in this book contain Scripture-based principles and perspective to help readers navigate differences, disagreements, and discomfort."

Vivian Mabuni, speaker, podcast host, founder of Someday
Is Here, and author of *Open Hands, Willing Heart*

"In *Come Sit with Me*, incredible women from all walks of life invite us to sit with them as they have hard conversations with Jesus and wrestle through issues of faith that we all can relate to. While reading this book there were several times I simply would say 'Amen!' because someone would speak specifically to an issue of my heart."

Jennifer Lucy Tyler, Bible teacher, founder of SoulCircles
Ministries, and national presenter for Logos Bible Software

come
sit
with
me

Books from (in)courage

For more resources, visit incourage.me.

come
sit
with
me

How to Delight in Differences, Love through Disagreements, and Live with Discomfort

(in)courage

Edited by Becky Keife

Revell

a division of Baker Publishing Group
Grand Rapids, Michigan

Published by Revell
a division of Baker Publishing Group
PO Box 6287, Grand Rapids, MI 49516-6287
www.revellbooks.com

Library of Congress Cataloging-in-Publication Data
Names: (in)courage (Organisation)
Title: Come sit with me : how to delight in differences, love through disagreements, and live with discomfort / (in)courage.
Description: Grand Rapids, MI : Revell, a division of Baker Publishing Group, [2022]
Identifiers: LCCN 2022970001 | ISBN 9780800738143 | ISBN 9780800742454 (casebound) | ISBN 9781493438778 (ebook)
Subjects: LCSH: Love—Religious aspects—Christianity. | Interpersonal relations—Religious aspects—Christianity.
Classification: LCC BV4639 .C5835 2022 | DDC 241/.4—dc23/eng/20220404
LC record available at https://lccn.loc.gov/2022970001

To protect the privacy of those who have shared their stories with the authors, some details and names have been changed.

(in)courage is represented by Alive Literary Agency, www.aliveliterary.com.

22 23 24 25 26 27 28   7 6 5 4 3 2 1

Contents

introduction

If You're Tempted to Give Up on People,
Read This

I can't believe she said/did/believes that.
The pain is too much.
The divide between us is too wide.
We'll never see eye to eye.
They don't understand me.
I'm tired of arguing.
We have nothing in common.
I haven't walked in their shoes, and they haven't walked
  in mine.
They aren't willing to try.
This is too hard.
I don't know what to say or where to start.
I'm not equipped to build that friendship.
It's impossible to repair this relationship.
I'm too hurt to move forward.

Have you ever had thoughts like one (or all) of these? Maybe you've even said something like this out loud? If so, you're not alone. Being human is hard. Being in relationships with other humans is even harder. And it just seems to be getting more complicated every day.

Sometimes the unspoken tensions between us make it difficult to breathe. The tiny fractures. Silent assumptions. Fresh wounds or decades of scars. A widening divide between sisters and brothers, husbands and wives, neighbors, coworkers, college roommates, online acquaintances, best of friends and could-be friends. Do you feel it? Do you know how to move through it?

We each come to the kitchen table, the bus stop, the office coffeepot, or the church potluck with our own gifts and our own junk. We carry the weight of past hurts, strong opinions, and well-founded fears. We also carry with us our unique and delightful differences. We show up to boardrooms and living rooms with our distinct languages and cultures, personality types and perspectives, experiences and convictions.

Both the beautiful and the broken parts of our stories can make connecting with others challenging—or sometimes infuriating, disheartening, or just plain impossible.

Have you felt this way? When it comes to difficult people, have you wanted to throw in the towel or build an impenetrable wall around your heart? Have you tried to avoid eye contact in Costco when you see that friend who is forever wanting to debate hot-button issues, or have you sent a phone call straight to voicemail because the risk of being manipulated or misunderstood again is just too much? Have you longed to be seen and accepted for who you are, but others just seem to want you to be someone you're not? If your answer to any of these questions is yes, you're in the right place, friend.

Your sisters at (in)courage know what it's like to feel frustrated in friendships. To feel fed up with the complexity of relationships in today's culture. We know what it's like to lose confidence in humanity while still clinging to a wisp of hope in the God who holds us all. We know what it's like to get it all wrong, to face our own failings, and to see Jesus meet us in our mess anyway.

Now more than ever, relationships feel anything but straightforward. What if taking the next step in your messy or complex relationship looked like just taking a seat?

For years, the writers of (in)courage have been sitting down together, virtually and in person, to wrestle through what it looks like to delight in our *differences* rather than ignore or abhor them. We've done the hard work of loving one another through *disagreements* and learning to live in the *discomfort* that naturally comes with being a bunch of beautifully imperfect, wildly distinct women. We are not flawless experts but battle-worn survivors who have seen the goodness of God in seemingly insurmountable situations; we're here to tell you about our heartaches and mistakes and hope in the one true God who hasn't given up on us.

In the pages ahead you'll find stories, ideas, and invitations. Rather than prescribing a formula for changing people or situations, *Come Sit with Me* offers twenty-six hope-filled guides to loving well in all circumstances. Together we'll ask:

- When relationships are complex, how do we learn to delight in our differences?

- When we disagree on issues or hold different positions, how do we still honor and value individuals?
- When hard truths and nuanced conversations are difficult to navigate, how do we connect before we correct?
- When people disappoint us, how do we keep trusting that God is working in every situation?
- When forgiveness feels impossible, how do we move forward?
- And ultimately, how do we live and love like Jesus—serving others, being slow to speak and quick to listen, extending humble generosity and authentic hospitality, and just sitting together?

The writers of (in)courage tackle these tough questions by going first with our own hard-fought, grace-filled learning moments. From politics to religious differences, from dealing with toxic people to dealing with our own unforgiveness and desire for revenge, we reveal the struggles no one wants to really talk about—and how we can actually grow closer to God and others through the circumstances we'd rather run from.

Whether you are in the middle of a conflict with no resolution, feel the ache of changing relationships, or wonder how to enter into a friend's pain, our stories will help you take a deep breath, show you you're not alone in the stress and mess, and serve as a gentle guide to letting God work through your disagreements, differences, and discomfort in ways you might never expect.

We know that no two stories are the same, so our prayer is that through these pages you will find the comfort of seeing glimpses of yourself in someone else's experience and also learn from experiences unlike your own. Each chapter ends with questions to sit with: three to ask yourself and three to ask God. Consider grabbing a notebook and choosing one (or all of them!) to journal through after each chapter. The quiet work of hope and transformation is possible when we're willing to sit with God and invite the Holy Spirit to move in us. It is possible to grow in love when we're willing to sit together.

The apostle Paul gave this sound advice about what it looks like to love well:

> Don't just pretend to love others. Really love them. Hate what is wrong. Hold tightly to what is good. Love each other with genuine affection, and take delight in honoring each other. Never be lazy, but work hard and serve the Lord enthusiastically. Rejoice in our confident hope. Be patient in trouble, and keep on praying. When God's people are in need, be ready to help them. Always be eager to practice hospitality.
>
> Bless those who persecute you. Don't curse them; pray that God will bless them. Be happy with those who are happy, and weep with those who weep. Live in harmony with each other. Don't be too proud to enjoy the company of ordinary people. And don't think you know it all! (Rom. 12:9–16 NLT)

What would it look like to live this out? How would our hearts change if we set aside arguing in comment threads and sat next to one another instead? How might our world change if we would all agree to be people who both celebrate and weep with our friends, coworkers, and neighbors before ever trying to convince, correct, or lobby our agendas?

Loving others isn't easy. Jesus never said it would be. But He did call us to do it, and therefore we know it will be worth it. "So now I am giving you a new commandment: Love each other. Just as I have loved you, you should love each other. Your love for one another will prove to the world that you are my disciples" (John 13:34–35 NLT).

And perhaps this love begins by just acknowledging the tension we feel and sitting in that tension together.

Come and sit with us.

Take this journey with friends!

Come Sit with Me is the perfect book to go through as a small group or book club. Use the questions at the end of each chapter to reflect on your own stories and share how God is working in your lives. You can also take advantage of "Questions to Ask When You're Sitting Together" at the end of the book. Choose a question or two each week to help break the ice with new friends or to go deeper with an established community of people.

1

Table of One

Jennifer Dukes Lee

C ome. Sit with me. Let's talk.
I'm in the booth to your left, the one tucked up against
the corner of the restaurant. There are a bunch of local folks
sitting on barstools, and their heads all swivel toward the door
when you walk in. You're new here.

I saved a seat for you across the table from me.

The seat is made of vinyl, and it makes a squeaking sound
when you slide across it. A single napkin is sticking out of
a plastic container, and when you pull the first one out, another pops up, just like a box of tissues. A sign on the wall
says, "Buy one hamburger for the price of two and receive a
second hamburger for free." That makes me smile.

It smells like fries and bacon, and the waitress brings two
glasses of water in tall mason jars.

I picked this table for a reason. I've sat here many times
with my husband when it seemed like we were worlds apart
on the issues of the day. Suffice it to say, he and I haven't
exactly seen eye to eye when we vote. But this is the table

where my husband and I sit after every political election to have dinner and conversation together. For as long as I can remember we've done this after leaving the polling place just up the street from here.

The polling place—it's where the roads of our marriage have diverged when our ink pens hover over tiny ovals on secret ballots.

Election after election, we walk into the polling place, cast our ballots, and walk out, side by side. In time, the awkwardness of this marital divide has softened, even when our differences haven't. We often joke on our way back to the car, "Did our votes cancel each other out again?" Sometimes they do; sometimes they don't.

But always we have come here, to this table.

Long ago we made the decision to break bread together in the form of a shared plate of buffalo wings. We talk. We listen. And yes, we even disagree. This has never been easy. There have been tears at this table—*mine*. There has been defensiveness and eye-rolling—*again, mine*. There have been uncomfortable conversations that we carry back through the front door into our home. But believe it or not, we have learned from each other at this table and have found common ground from time to time.

Whenever I think about this table, it gives me hope.

And that's why I invited you here—to talk and to hope.

Come Sit with Me and Learn Together

Maybe you don't want to sit with me. Maybe you're wondering who I voted for all those times when my husband I and drove to the polling place, and maybe you're not so sure you want to be seen with someone like me.

Then again, maybe you *do* want to sit here. Maybe you've been feeling like no one has room at the table for you anymore because of the way you feel about politics, parenting, climate change, alcoholic beverages, policing, critical race theory, religion, science, divorce, international adoption, vaccines, or public education. The list is unending.

Chances are, you are living in the tension of being misunderstood. And maybe these days you feel rejected or abandoned. Without warning, you lost a treasured friendship that fractured over a difference of opinion. You just found out your next-door neighbor unfriended you last week.

If there's a way forward, the path feels hidden.

My grandfather said there were two things you should never talk about at the dining room table: religion and politics.

And then came 2020. All of a sudden, that's all anybody wanted to talk about: religion and politics—along with masks and vaccines and social distancing and police practices and racial relations. And everywhere we looked, everyone was arguing. For many of us, 2020 was the year our differences came into sharp relief.

It got heated at the table, didn't it? Chairs screeched back on the hardwood floor. Voices pitched higher. People blocked, unfriended, and canceled their way into their own little echo chambers. We looked for churches and neighborhoods where everyone else thought and voted and behaved just like us, because that felt safer.

But ignoring our differences doesn't actually make anything safer. It just makes us more insulated and divided.

And let's be honest: few places felt safe. Even the family Thanksgiving table suddenly turned into a battlefield. You realized that you didn't even see eye to eye with people you love dearly. Yet you didn't have the option of unfriending your spouse, best friend, sister-in-law, or children. These are your people, and you just want to figure out how to live in peace with them.

But is it possible? Can we actually live in peace with someone we greatly disagree with? Can we find common ground when tiny fractures have already widened into canyons?

God must have known that we would need help navigating seasons of discord and divisiveness. The Old Testament is filled with stories of war, conflict, and conquest, and in the New Testament we read of heated debates over Jesus's teachings. But the Bible is not a story where disagreement has the final say.

The Bible is a story where Jesus extends us all an irresistible invitation: "Come. Sit with Me at the table." It wasn't an invitation for only those who wore the right clothes or checked the right ballot boxes or lived a righteous life.

It was—and is—an invitation for us all.

Before His death, Jesus extended that kind of invitation at a Passover meal. His friends showed up, and they all reclined at the table. Among them was the betrayer, Judas Iscariot. Jesus's invitation for Judas to sit at the table is an astounding expression of friendship and love.

In John 13, there's this heart-stopping moment at the supper table when Jesus tells His disciples that one of them will betray Him. The disciples stare at one another, at a loss over what Jesus could mean. John finally asks, "Lord, who is it?" (v. 25).

"Jesus answered, 'It is the one to whom I will give this piece of bread when I have dipped it in the dish.' Then, dipping the piece of bread, he gave it to Judas, the son of Simon Iscariot" (v. 26).

This action of dipping bread and giving it to a person at the table was a common cultural practice. But don't miss this: it was a way to single out *the honored guest* at the table, similar to someone standing up to give a toast at a wedding reception. It was a mark of esteem, as if Jesus was saying to His betrayer, "I love you. I honor you. I raise a toast to you."

I have to ask myself, Would I be okay inviting someone to dinner who is part of a plot to kill me? Would I be able to share a table with someone who rabidly dislikes me? Would I raise a toast to a person who I personally find offensive and disagreeable? Would I consider my enemy an honored guest?

I want to find myself answering yes to those questions, but if I'm being honest, I haven't always been able to do that.

It's tempting for me to say, "Well, it was easier for Jesus. He was fully human, but He was also fully God, and with God's perfect love coursing through His whole being, Jesus was able to do something that I simply cannot do." Or, shall I say, *will not do?*

Yet, God doesn't give us a pass when it comes to loving our adversaries. Jesus says it plainly: "Love your enemies" (Matt. 5:44). And I don't think this love is an "I'll love you at a distance" kind of love. Rather, it's an up-close-and-personal, welcome-to-my-table love. The Greek word translated here as "love" is *agape*, which is the highest form of love. *Unconditional* love. I have to ask myself what it looks like to love my enemy with the highest form of love—with genuine delight, goodwill, and charity.

Check out Paul's instructions to the Colossians:

Therefore, as God's chosen people, holy and dearly loved, clothe yourselves with compassion, kindness, humility, gentleness and patience. Bear with each other and forgive one another if any of you has a grievance against someone. Forgive as the Lord forgave you. And over all these virtues put on love, which binds them all together in perfect unity. (Col. 3:12–14)

Nowhere does he say to walk away from those we disagree with. Nowhere does he say to avoid people or retreat into echo chambers where we can hear only reverberations of our own viewpoint and opinions. He doesn't say to block or unfriend, to cancel or discount another person. Instead he calls us to forgive one another, to choose compassion, have patience, and "bear with each other." In the original Greek, that little phrase doesn't simply mean to put up with or to tolerate. It means to endure, to have patience with, and—get this—*to suffer.*

Bearing with one another can feel like suffering, can't it? Yet this is the way of Christ. We are called to sit close enough to people that they could reach over and hurt us. That's exactly what Jesus did. He kept His betrayer close enough to hand him a piece of bread.

As we sit here, you and I, at this table, I am wondering if this is how we begin. Right here. Together. And then, what if we could step across party lines, religious lines, personality lines, and invite more people to join us?

I can't stop thinking about how little time each of us has on earth to fulfill God's call for unity—a call issued many centuries ago. Before He goes to the cross, Jesus spends some of His last precious moments on earth praying for His disciples and for future believers—us! Twice in John 17 He prays for unity among us. "Holy Father, protect them by the power of your name, the name you gave me, *so that they may be one as we are one*" (v. 11, emphasis added). He repeats the prayer in verses 20–21: "I pray . . . that all of them may be one." The early church decided unity was a worthy calling. Fast-forward to the book of Acts, where we're told, "All the believers were one in heart and mind" (Acts 4:32). We know they did not agree on every issue that arose; they were humans just like us, after all. But they understood what unified them—Jesus. Jesus broke down every barrier for Jew and gentile alike, a radical change in ideology that took time for everyone to embrace, but the early church eventually got there.

Now, it's our time.

Here's what we risk if we don't find a way forward: we will each end up sitting at a table of one.

If we have to agree with every single person in our church on every single issue, we will be sitting in a church of one.

If we have to agree with our neighbor on every single issue, we will live in a neighborhood of one.

A book club of one. A Bible study of one. A living room of one. A family of one.

We're all going to sit alone at Thanksgiving and Christmas and even the communion table where Jesus beckons us to "Take and eat." A table of one.

I know how uncomfortable it is. Every election cycle, every news story, and every political event has the potential to set off fireworks in my own home—and not the pretty kind but the explosive, cover-your-ears-and-run-for-cover kind.

But my husband and I have finally come to a place where our divisions no longer shock us. In the same way, our global divisions should not shock us.

Scott and I got married knowing full well that we didn't always agree. But we got married anyway. Here's why: because we loved "us" more than we hated what was different.

That conviction is what keeps us coming to this table twenty-five years later. Maybe that's a starting place for each of us today: We can love "us" more than we hate what is different.

I understand how hard this is, but silence isn't working (and neither is shouting on Facebook). I know of friends who haven't talked in more than a year because of divisions over recent events. These friends used to sit at the same table, vacation together, worship together. As days turn to months turn to years, that gap will continue to widen unless it's dealt with.

Maybe we could try this instead.

Instead of unfriending that college roommate with her unending rants on social media, use the Facebook Like button to let her know you love the photo of her kid holding up his new driver's license.

Instead of arguing with your dad over how he voted, listen as he tells you what he's been thinking. (We can listen without agreeing and still enjoy the Thanksgiving turkey!)

This doesn't mean that the hot-button issues aren't important. They are. But if our divisions create an all-or-nothing mentality, then we're all missing out. So instead of focusing on everything that divides, let's find points of connection. We might not agree with the way our next-door neighbors parent their children, but when we get to know them, we might realize that we both share a fondness for historical fiction and sushi.

I understand that sushi won't save the world. And I know that this vinyl booth tucked into the corner of a small-town restaurant won't right all the wrongs.

But like the old song says, "Let there be peace on earth, and let it begin with me."

And with you.

Right here, at our table of two.

Questions to Sit With

Ask Yourself

1. How has the call to "bear with each other" felt like suffering?

2. Is it possible for a human being to love an enemy with unconditional agape love? If so, how?

3. Who could I invite to the table, giving him or her an opportunity to talk, while my main job is to listen?

Ask God

1. Lord, how have I refused to love and value people in my life when we disagree?

2. Where in my life am I at risk of becoming a table of one?

3. Jesus, show me how to love like You love—even those who've betrayed me. Help me to love Your call to unity more than I hate what divides me from my neighbor.

Mending a Marriage That Was Falling Apart

Grace P. Cho

We sat awkwardly side by side on the black leather couch in our living room, the quiet of a sleeping house amplifying the silence between us. For months our marriage had been falling apart at the seams, and everything we had built over ten years seemed to be dissolving faster than we could pull it back together. Where there had once been understanding and shared laughter, we now had only disbelief and sharp words for each other. I used to say that the greatest thing about our marriage was that we were friends, but after an unplanned career change unearthed buried resentments and misperceived expectations, we had become strangers—angry, unforgiving, and exhausted with each other.

What was there left to say at this point? Every interaction had become fraught with tension, meanness, and hopelessness. And though we were in marriage counseling, the real work at home of learning to communicate and listen, of trying to mend what felt beyond repair, was draining. I had nothing left in me anymore—no more energy to keep going, to even hope that things could get better—and I didn't know how much longer I could do this.

The continued silence made the air still and stuffy. Neither of us knew what to say, and with our polar opposite personalities—me as the verbal, reflective processor, and him as the unexpressive, logical one—we were at an impasse. Someone had to break the silence, and as much as I resisted being the one to put into practice what we had learned in therapy, I asked the question he needed to hear: "What are you feeling?"

I knew to be ready for the minutes of no response while he formulated his thoughts into emotions and then into words. I could think of a million things to say as I waited for an answer, but my growth edge, unlike his, was learning to be patient and giving him the space to take his time. So I bit my sharp tongue and waited, expecting the worst.

Finally, he said, "I don't feel seen."

For once I was the one without words. That was exactly how he had made me feel for so many years. How could our pains be the same? How could we both feel unseen and unknown by the other? I tried to think of ways I had failed at seeing him for who he is, how I might not have been loving or supportive, but I couldn't pinpoint exact moments.

Instead of trying to guess, I asked, "How do you feel unseen by me?"

He began sharing, and as he did, one story led to another, one step at a time into the past, until it became clear he'd felt this sense of invisibility since he was a child.

From my perspective, he had been his family's golden child—the one everyone looked up to, the one who could never do anything wrong, the one who had it all together. He seemed highly visible, cared for, and loved unconditionally. And yet, from where he stood, he felt he could be only what his loved ones expected him to be—and that included me. It was as though his goodness shrouded who he really was—a human being who has thoughts and feelings that go unexpressed because the world turns at a speed that is often beyond him.

The strange thing was, I also had felt invisible since childhood, lost among my siblings and visible only when I'd get in trouble. I had learned from my experience that being good and proper could get me the attention I sought, but I just couldn't seem to be good enough.

Now here we were as adults, having grown up with the same wound and hurting each other in the exact ways we'd been hurt. I shook my head at the irony.

We had felt as though we couldn't possibly understand each other; we just didn't know how much we could.

Our tense bodies exhaled in the shared pain. I scooted over to close the gap between us that had felt like an abyss we'd never be able to cross. There was still so much to heal in our marriage, but this felt like the beginning of hope. Perhaps if we could understand each other better, we'd be able to see each other with clearer, kinder eyes. Then we could learn to love with tenderness again.

I leaned over and rested my head on his arm. He took my hand, and we sat together, quiet and still.

Come Sit with Me and Learn Together

I look back on that time in our marriage, and the memories still sting my heart like tiny cactus needles. We survived falling apart, but mending the mess was a slow, pain-filled process. We recognized how we had intentionally hidden parts of ourselves, assuming the other person wouldn't understand and would therefore reject us. We noticed our patterns of communication, paid attention to what triggered our pain points, and examined the beliefs we had about ourselves, each other, and the world. We faithfully attended our therapy sessions, which included lots of tears, occasional yelling, and working through the same problems again and again.

I often wondered, then, if it was worth it—worth being in the marriage, worth putting in the effort for an outcome I wasn't guaranteed, worth keeping at it when I couldn't even imagine what a future together might look like. And the only thing that kept me grounded was the redeeming power of the gospel. If miraculous and impossible things can happen in Christ, such as resurrection from the dead, surely there was hope for us in our marriage. Surely we could change for the better, and it would be worth it to wait and see what God might do.

In Matthew 19:26, Jesus says, "With man this is impossible, but with God all things are possible." Though this verse has been used too flippantly in the church as a way to gloss over difficult circumstances, during that season of marital hardship, I held on to it for the promise that it is. It anchored me in hope, giving me the sustenance I needed to try and commit to our marriage for another day, another month, another year.

Mending a marriage or any other relationship is not always possible, but when it is, the hardest part can be doing the simplest things, like having a conversation, asking questions, and staying curious about the other person to get to know them better.

Isn't that what we all want? To be fully known? Wholly seen?

Even though my husband has thoughts and emotions beyond what he shows, it's difficult for him to access them and find the words to express them. By asking him directly about his feelings, I give him the opportunity to stay present with himself, figure out how to describe what he's feeling, and then verbalize his thoughts to me. By asking questions, I open the door for him to take up space, be himself as much as possible, and create connections between us.

The questions will vary based on different relationships and situations, but the key to asking the right ones is to stay curious, which is different from being nosy. Curiosity keeps us tender to each other's humanity.

When we don't know someone, it's easy to dehumanize them and treat them as if they're an object made for our judgment. We can make assumptions about their character, their background, their family, their life, and feel justified as we do so. But when we stay curious, we keep their humanity in view. Curiosity helps us remember that the person we share a home with and the acquaintance on Facebook are both individuals made and loved by God. We may not agree or have the same values. We may never become close with that other mom at school or that neighbor across the street, but we can genuinely care for one another. We might even find that we laugh at the same things or have similar passions. We might learn we have a shared pain or we're on a similar journey in life. And perhaps then, even when all hope feels lost, we can take small steps toward mending the gaps created by our differences.

Questions to Sit With

Ask Yourself

1. In my difficult or strained relationships, how can the power of the gospel give me hope?
2. In what ways have I dehumanized people, and how can I stay curious and tender toward them?
3. What is one small step I can take toward mending a relationship with someone where our differences have created a rift?

Ask God

1. Lord, in what areas of my life or heart have I become too hardened to believe that all things are possible with You?
2. What are the barriers within my heart and mind that keep me from wanting to mend the relationships that need mending?
3. God, who are the people in my life that You're inviting me to try to love again?

3

What If Pain Is the Stage for Miracles?

Becky Keife

There was a time in my life when my parents couldn't be in the same room with each other. As a kid, I learned to wait on the wicker love seat and stare impatiently out the big picture window. (Yes, it was the early nineties and we had wicker furniture in the living room.) As soon as I saw my dad's black sedan pull into the driveway, I would yell to my sisters that it was time to go and we would race out the front door. Was I that excited to see my dad? Honestly, not really. I was just that eager to avoid him coming up to the house and igniting a possible confrontation with my mom.

In middle school, I remember standing up for my trumpet solo and quickly scanning the crowded gymnasium in search of supportive faces. I spotted my mom in the left set of bleachers and my dad in the farthest possible section to the right. In high school, when I got the lead in *Oklahoma*, my parents came to different shows, careful not to cross paths lest a community theater become a battleground.

There were a thousand spoken and unspoken hurts between my parents that spilled over into my heart. The way my dad wouldn't help pay for my sister's dance classes to make life harder for my mom. The way my mom didn't hide her disdain for the summer vacations my dad took us girls on, which made me feel like my excitement was a betrayal. Fifteen years of marriage in and as many years of bitterness out. I never knew if their divorce was the right choice, the only choice. As a kid I never longed for them to get back together—I just wanted things to be different. I just wanted to escape the shrapnel of their pain.

At my college graduation, my dad pretended not to hear me when I asked him to stand next to me for a picture with our whole family—the original five. When I was getting married, my mom didn't want to sit *beside* my dad and his new wife; my dad didn't want to sit in the row *behind* my mom. Several verbal blowups and low blows left me gutted. Three days before my big day, I looked at my wedding dress hanging on the closet door and wondered if my dad would even show up to walk me down the aisle.

I share all this not as a catalog of grievances against my parents but to set the stage for the miracle I never expected.

Fast-forward several years to when my dad was in a difficult place in his life—well, difficult is an understatement. His second marriage had failed, as had his business and his health. Thanksgiving was approaching. Holidays are always extra complicated for kids of divorce. My sisters and I were all married at this point and had to juggle time with our in-laws and separate gatherings for our mom and dad. Now that my dad was single and struggling, the responsibility to host a celebration with him fell to one of us girls—an added stress when our individual lives were already maxed and being with Dad didn't feel especially celebratory.

The details of what happened next have become a bit fuzzy through the fog of years. The question might have come through an email or group text thread, or maybe we were talking on the phone while I nursed a baby. Either way, I'll never forget my mom's words: "How would you feel if I invited your dad to join us for Thanksgiving?"

As I sat there speechless, my mom went on to explain how she understood what a burden it was to navigate three family get-togethers and how the busyness could take away from the joy of the holiday. She said she wasn't sure if Dad would accept an invitation from her, but she felt like the Lord was asking her to extend it.

Honestly? My first thought was *No way!* I pictured the awkwardness of being in the same house *all* together. I thought about how I would take the chaos of bouncing from one Thanksgiving dinner to the next to the next over the tension of sitting at the same table with my parents for an extended meal. The family chasm caused by their divorce was way too wide to bridge with some mashed potatoes and gravy. Years and years of conflict and failed resolutions proved that reconciliation was impossible, right? So why even try?

Given our family history, this knee-jerk reaction was understandable—but it was also rooted in fear. I'm grateful to tell you that my initial response didn't win out.

The first miracle was my mom asking my dad to Thanksgiving dinner. The second miracle was the doorbell ringing and my dad showing up in his classic corduroy slacks and argyle sweater and handing my mom a bottle of Martinelli's. The miracles after that were too many to count.

As little ones threw corn kernels from high chairs and unspoken words passed in sideways glances between sisters, we made it through that first Thanksgiving dinner. My dad thanked my mom for inviting him and complimented her cooking. My mom thanked my dad for coming and gave him another piece of homemade pie to go. It felt a bit like I was living someone else's life.

It was hard and uncomfortable and so very worth it. I left that dinner with a belly full of turkey and a heart full of praise. What I thought was surely impossible turned out not to be. From our pain God produced a miracle—and I'm still giving thanks.

Come Sit with Me and Learn Together

That Thanksgiving dinner was the first of many times my mom and dad would sit together at the same holiday table. After that, there was a standing invitation for my dad to join our family celebrations. And I never want to get over the miracle of it. I never want to lose sight of the fact that what took place over plates of green beans and baskets of bread was the work of the Holy Spirit—and a bunch of messed-up people willing to surrender to the gift of His leading.

Think about it: My mom could have ignored the Spirit's stirring. Pain and resentment could have blocked her from extending an offering of peace and compassion. My dad could have rejected the invitation. Pride and bitterness could have been barriers to reconciliation and connection.

My sisters and I could have dismissed the hope of family harmony. Anger and unforgiveness for the turmoil caused by our parents' fractured marriage could have prevented the miracle God wanted to do in our family. I could have said the pain of the past was already too much to bear, so why open myself to the possibility of more?

There are a dozen or more reasons why that first family dinner should never have happened following fifteen years of brutal divorce aftermath. But God . . . (Oh, those two small and mighty words.)

But God was working for the good of those who love Him. And that's the wild thing about what His Word promises! "And we know that in all things God works for the good of those who love him, who have been called according to his purpose" (Rom. 8:28).

Did you catch that? *All things*. God doesn't just use the moments of our lives that we deem worthy of an Instagram highlight reel. He doesn't reserve His work only for the times when we get things right, when we walk without stumbling, when we run without being wounded by the pain of our own making. He works *all* things together for our good. The only qualifier is that we love Him.

I showed up to that unexpected Thanksgiving dinner still carrying old wounds crusted over with the scab of time. I came with my guard partly up and plenty of skepticism stuffed in my back pocket. But I came to the table. And so did my mother, my father, and my sisters. Sometimes just showing up is the beginning to building new bridges of connection. Showing up with a hefty dose of humility helps.

Humility says I'm willing to give the other person the benefit of the doubt.

Humility says being right or even being heard is not the most important thing.

Humility says I'm going to do my best to love well regardless of how someone else chooses to respond.

I didn't hear those exact words come out of anyone's mouth that November night, but each person's actions spoke volumes. And God's voice in our midst was the loudest. I'm not sure who else heard Him, but I couldn't ignore the tender, relentless assurance of the Spirit saying, *See Me. See how I'm doing the impossible. See how I'm answering prayers you didn't even know to pray. See how I'm infusing hope and life and healing into your family in ways you never could have imagined.*

Perhaps that's what the Holy Spirit is whispering to you today. Maybe He's urging you to take a close look at what Paul says about how God meets us in our places of weakness:

And the Holy Spirit helps us in our weakness. For example, we don't know what God wants us to pray for. But the Holy Spirit prays for us with groanings that cannot be expressed in words. And the Father who knows all hearts knows what the Spirit is saying, for the Spirit pleads for us believers in harmony with God's own will. (Rom. 8:26–27 NLT)

Growing up in a divorced and dysfunctional family certainly seemed like a weakness. Feeling powerless in navigating emotionally charged relationships with my parents usually left me bleary with tears and hopelessness. Often I didn't even know how to pray. Yet I see now with hope-restored clarity that God never left me. He was working on my behalf all along.

If you look at a circumstance or relationship in your life and feel *sure* that the pain and strife of today will always be this way; if you've lost hope that any glimmer of redemption is possible because the rift of bitterness and unforgiveness runs too deep; if you think the people in your life will never be able to change—that you'll never be able to let go, move forward, find healing—ask the Holy Spirit to groan on your behalf. Ask the God of the impossible, the God of the unimaginable to intercede. He just might want to give you an opportunity to extend an unexpected invitation, accept one, or simply show up.

Friend, I don't know what relational bridges in your life feel too broken to rebuild. I don't know what emotional injuries from the past are still wreaking havoc on your heart or your holidays. But I know that God is with you. I know that what seems impossible today *can* change by His power. I also know that He asks us to partner with Him. He asks us to come with love and humility. To follow His lead and open our hearts to the possibility that He just might want to do more than we could ask or imagine. It won't always be comfortable. The tension might be thicker than your mom's lumpy gravy. But sitting together with a shared, tender hope for a fresh outpouring of healing and grace is worth it.

It has now been ten years since my dad passed away. The last time I ever saw him was at our family Christmas gathering—miracle upon miracle.

Questions to Sit With

Ask Yourself

1. What circumstance or relationship feels hopeless or impossible to repair?
2. What barriers or blockades exist within my own heart that are keeping me from healing past hurts or making new connections?
3. Who can I initiate with this week? Who can I love without expecting a loving response in return?

Ask God

1. Lord, where has pain, pride, resentment, bitterness, or unforgiveness taken root in my life?
2. How do You want me to show up to relationships with humility right now?
3. Holy Spirit, speak to me and guide me! I'm listening. What do You want to say or do in my difficult relationships? I surrender my past, present, and future to You.

4

Setting Seats at the Table for My Political Opponents

Michelle Ami Reyes

I don't think your political stance is biblical."

I had just finished giving a talk on politics to a group of college students. Over the course of the hour I had been questioned about my stance on a number of the big issues of the day, and I had tried my best to interweave Scripture with my own personal experiences to offer what I hoped were nuanced approaches on everything from who to vote for to questions about immigration, homeland security, the pro-life movement, racism, and more. However, after the forum, one woman approached me with a determined look on her face. She was visibly upset, and before I even realized it, my body began to tense up. I was preparing for a fight.

The woman went on to share where she personally stood on the issues discussed during that evening's forum and how she didn't believe the Scripture passages I referenced supported what I was advocating for politically. As I felt my heart begin to pound a bit faster, I reminded myself to stop and take a deep breath. I didn't know this woman and she didn't know me, but here she was arguing that not only did she disagree with my political stances but that they were unbiblical as well. I knew I needed to be calm before responding to her critique.

To be honest, this is why conversations about politics can be so hard with fellow brothers and sisters in the Lord. When we disagree politically, we're quick to criticize the other person's interpretation of Scripture, even accuse each other of heresy. These conversations can escalate quickly, and hurt often boils over into anger and defensiveness. I knew I needed to not take this woman's words personally, even though her aggressive tone and posture were hard to swallow.

Granted, I'm not one to shy away from hard conversations. I even welcome different opinions. But this woman was angry, and as our conversation went on her words became more aggressive. I could feel my own frustration rising as I wondered, *Why is she attacking me? Did she not hear everything I just shared in my talk? Did she not hear the Scripture passages I quoted? Why is she so angry, anyways? Can't we just calmly discuss our opinions on these issues together?*

When someone begins outright attacking me, I don't always feel the need to engage. Sometimes the godliest response is to not say anything at all, or to respectfully thank them for their thoughts and move on. But this time I felt God tugging on my heart to respond differently. This person lived in my city; she moved and breathed in the same community I did. Even though she acted openly hostile, I got the feeling that there was more going on under the surface.

Her approach felt off, but I had a hunch that her heart was genuinely seeking answers.

So I asked, "Hey, would you be up for meeting in person and talking about this more?"

She came over a few weeks later, and we sat at my kitchen table with two hot cups of chai and some colorful bowls of cookies, grapes, and dates. Food is my love language, and even through my humble assortment of refreshments I wanted to communicate to this woman, "I want to be your friend and have hard but grace-filled conversations with you."

After a few sips of chai, I looked up and asked her, "So, how are you?"

Almost immediately she broke down in tears. "Not good," she said. She had fears—deep fears—about some of the big political issues of the day, and she felt like no one was listening to her. When I had gone up to speak at the college forum and she saw folks in the audience all nodding their heads, she felt alone and frustrated and helpless.

"I just feel like there's always two sides to an issue, but no one sees my side of things," she added.

I had not expected this response from her. I had expected a more detailed argument, more anger, but not this—not a hurting woman who was confused and in pain and just wanting to be understood. Immediately my own posture shifted. Admittedly, I had come prepared with more Scripture passages and talking points to justify my positions, but now none of that seemed to matter. Now the only thing that felt important was letting this weeping woman know that I cared about her enough to hear her side of things.

What followed was a beautiful hour of swapping stories, cataloging painful experiences, and relating personal journeys that have led us to see the world the way we do. I told the woman at my kitchen table, "I care about you and what you've gone through. I understand why you think the way you do. I still disagree on some of these issues, but I hope you better understand why I think the way I do, and I also hope we can be friends."

She smiled and said, "That would be great."

In that moment, I knew I had just made a new friend. We didn't see the world the same way, but that was okay. What was more important was that each of us gave the other the dignity of being heard and understood and even valued for our perspective. In the span of an afternoon around a table, we had been able to give that to each other. By the time she left there was no residual anger or hostility, only peace and gratefulness.

Come Sit with Me and Learn Together

It's far too easy to lose friends over opposing political stances. Maybe you've experienced a fractured friendship or someone has simply stopped talking to you because of your different views. I've been there and it's painful. But I've come to understand that while I can't change the other person's heart, I can certainly take responsibility for my own.

Whenever we find ourselves in conversation with someone who thinks differently about anything from voting to immigration to racism, we must first stop and remind ourselves: this person is not my enemy. Ephesians 6:12 says that we wage war not against people made of flesh and blood but against principalities and the rulers of darkness in this world.

In other words, we are called to fight the good battle of faith, not a battle of words. When we feel there is a force set against us, we shouldn't look at the person across from us and engage in a fleshly battle of shame, vengeance, or rejection. Rather, we are called to set our focus on God and respond to the situation with prayer, love, and biblical wisdom.

When people are openly spouting hostile words toward you because of what you believe, remember that Jesus loved His enemies and you can follow His example to love those who position themselves as your enemy. Like Jesus modeled, we can choose to bless those who persecute us and pray for those who hate us. By loving our supposed political adversaries, we open the door to an unexpected friendship where we can stand together in our common struggle against the true evils of this world.

That said, when someone is vehemently opposed to our political beliefs, they may *feel* like an enemy. But one of Jesus's most revolutionary teachings was to love our enemies. In Matthew 5:43–44 He tells us, "You have heard the law that says, 'Love your neighbor' and hate your enemy. But I say, love your enemies! Pray for those who persecute you!" (NLT). It's particularly challenging to love our political opponents when we feel the stakes are high. But regardless of our stances, we are all divine image-bearers. Remembering this is the beginning of learning to truly love those we disagree with.

One of the most powerful ways I have learned to show the kindness and love of Jesus is by reaching out to a friend, colleague, family member, or even a new acquaintance I clash with politically, and sitting down together over coffee or a meal and listening to each other. Imagine if we all did this. What if we did a better job of asking more questions and understanding the convictions of others and not just always talking about our own opinions? When hard truths and nuanced conversations are difficult to navigate, let's challenge ourselves to connect before we correct.

I love how Rondell Trevino, director and founder of the Immigration Coalition, puts it: "Jesus wants the world to see Christians loving one another even if they disagree politically. Jesus does NOT want the world to see Christians hating one another because they disagree politically. Why? Because the world will think Christians are united by politics, not Jesus."[1] In other words, you can be a Republican and still love your Democratic neighbor. You can be a Democrat and still love your Republican neighbor. As believers, we can take different political stances and still show the love of Christ to one another. Our aim should be for the world to know we are Christians by our love.

Moreover, let's learn to collaborate with people we disagree with. We have to do more than just barely tolerate each other. Jesus collaborated with both the conservatives and progressives of His day. He ate with both Pharisees and Zealots, as well as with tax collectors and sinners. He talked with them, engaged with them, welcomed them. We can do the same.

Let's make space for fellow brothers and sisters who don't agree with our personal opinions and political leanings. Let's invite others to share their experiences and convictions even when we believe their stances are unbiblical.

We can choose to love instead of shun, and we can choose to lean in and help instead of refuse to be involved in a cause

---

1. Rondell Trevino (@Rondell_Trevino), "Jesus wants the world to see Christians loving one another," Twitter, June 18, 2021, 7:46 p.m., https://twitter.com /rondell_trevino/status/1406035656728580097.

simply because someone thinks differently from us. The example of Jesus compels us to collaborate and build bridges, and this includes our fellow image-bearers with whom we disagree politically.

Questions to Sit With

Ask Yourself

1. Who are the people in my life that I find it challenging to have conversations with about politics?
2. How does my heart and body respond to political arguments? What are gentle ways I can become more mindful of my own physical and emotional responses?
3. Who is someone I disagree with politically that I can invite over for a meal this week? In what ways can I intentionally show this person that I love them because they are made in the image of God?

Ask God

1. Lord, how can I be slower to speak and quicker to listen when it comes to conversations around politics?
2. Holy Spirit, I need You. Help me to not see people I disagree with politically as my enemies.
3. God, what are some simple statements and questions I can use to communicate my love for another person even when I disagree with them?

5

When Forgiveness Is Exhausting

Lucretia Berry

M ost folks in my friend circle describe me as friendly, kindhearted, encouraging, and upbeat. I concur. Generally, my hope-filled, faith-fueled drive presents as a seemingly selfless and sunny disposition.

When it comes to other people, I typically believe the best and hope for the best. So much so that I've been asked, "How do you pretend to do that?" But honestly, I'm not faking it. Most of the time I genuinely have a childlike outlook, which is not something I personally cultivated. I can't take credit or share life hacks on how to cultivate such a propensity. I think I am hardwired this way.

Yet, in the recesses of my intrinsically positive point of view, behind the inner walls and in the rarely visited coves of my heart, I struggle with unforgiveness. The struggle is severe—a danger to my well-being. This makes no sense to me! How can I believe and think the best about other people, but then when someone intentionally tramples on me, it's

"Bye-bye brilliant, logical, mild-mannered Dr. Bruce Banner. Hello, impulsive, erratic Incredible Hulk!" I become a monster fixed on vengeance.

Several years ago, a leader in my community called me into her office, positioned herself across from me, and began an interrogation. Someone had led her to misinterpret something I'd said, and she conjured up a crazy story casting me as the villain. This leader then used concocted evidence to condemn me and was convinced I should be heavily penalized. To say I was blindsided and stunned by her false accusations would be an understatement. I greatly admired and respected this woman, had often spoken highly of her, and had even tried to emulate her. Therefore, I was brokenhearted—paralyzed—by the perceived joy she took in tormenting me from her position of power.

As she spewed threats, I cried excessively. Drained, deeply wounded, and bewildered, I dragged myself home to my one-bedroom apartment. Alone and sulking, I began sobbing out a prayer—a prayer for REVENGE! I cried out for my gracious, kind, and merciful God to avenge me. I actually prayed, "God, how are You going to get back at her for what she did to me?" Can you believe that? You see, my struggle to forgive those who intentionally harm me is real! But there in my bedroom, in the midst of my excruciating, suffocating pain, where murderous thoughts tasted like sweet justice amid bitter tears, where the hurt accessed the massive, ugly monster parts of my humanity, God's presence gently interrupted.

Sweetly, calmly, and omnipotently, God spoke: "You can forgive her."

I wish I could tell you that I instantly expressed gratitude to God and my desire for retaliation was resolved. Nope!

Instead, I was offended that God would speak of forgiveness while I was in so much pain. By my account, the woman who had wronged me needed to suffer. I wanted her to be fired, not forgiven.

Though injured and now insulted, I somehow managed to piece together a few life-giving words and fashion a prayer for my offender that more closely reflected the character of God. I asked God to bless her and to deliver her from the painful circumstances that had prompted her to falsely accuse and hurt me. But *forgiving* her would be an entirely different endeavor that seemed impossible at the time.

The wound seemed too massive to ever heal. The pain felt embedded in my psyche. Anger was infused into every part of my soul. I could not will myself to forgive her. I did not *want* to forgive her. Although I knew forgiveness was in my best interests, my pain made me reason that she did not deserve my forgiveness. I wanted to be free of the overwhelming resentment I felt toward her. But again, was it even possible to recover from this kind of relational destruction, to break free from the bondage of bitterness that entangled my soul? It sure didn't feel like it.

Come Sit with Me and Learn Together

My road to liberation would be lengthy, arduous, and tumultuous.

I tried all the things that have been prescribed to foster forgiveness. I prayed blessings for her. I read all the Scripture passages about how we've been forgiven so we should now forgive. I listened to great messages that outlined formulas for forgiveness. I journaled to get my pain on paper and out of my head. I considered her pain and tried to empathize with her so as not to take her attack personally, because "hurt people hurt people." I did it all, yet relief did not come.

The path to forgiveness was exhausting. I felt like I was wrestling a mammoth, prehistoric, octopus-like creature. I was overwhelmed by the enormity of its grabby tentacles that squeezed and sucked the life out of me. It was a losing battle. The more effort I put toward forgiving, the more I felt the sting of unforgiveness. And failure to conquer the unforgiveness monster only compounded my unforgiveness with shame. Perhaps you have heard this familiar adage by Marianne Williamson: "Unforgiveness is like drinking poison yourself and waiting for the other person to die."[1] Well, drinking the poison seemed easier than exerting the strength to forgive. And because the offense was so painful, the poison of unforgiveness did not even taste toxic.

But inside my poisoned heart, I was terrified that unforgiveness would be the death of me, that somehow I'd be discounted in God's eyes. It didn't seem fair or logical that I had been burdened with the responsibility of forgiveness. But what felt like a burden was actually an invitation to know God's love in the form of patience, compassion, commitment, and consistence.

Cultivating patience, compassion, commitment, and consistence is not prioritized or primarily sought after in our culture of instant gratification. We don't want to be patient. We don't want to persevere in navigating interactions with

1. Marianne Williamson, QuoteNova.net, https://www.quotenova.net/authors/marianne-williamson/q2w396.

those who wound us. I'm sure you know what I mean. When your soul has been deeply injured, you want immediate relief from the pain. You don't want to have to figure out what to say the next time you are in the room with that longtime, trusted friend who betrayed you. You don't want to have to continue working under the revered leader who spiritually abused you. You just want to detach from the source of your pain. The desire to flee is understandable because it is a natural psychological response of protection. Trust me, I've been there. But disengaging from the pain is not the only thing necessary for our healing.

When avoidance isn't possible and relief from your pain isn't immediate, remember that you have been graced with *time*.

Over time—and I mean many, many years—the unforgiveness monster loosened its choke hold on me. Little by little its tentacles released their grip, or maybe I grew stronger in my ability to resist. Perhaps both. Either way, the change was so subtle, so gradual, I almost didn't feel it until I realized I was actually free.

I realized that I needed time more than I needed to implement a forgiveness formula. God met me in my stifled unforgiveness and gifted me with unhurried space to process. God stayed with me, and together we cultivated seeds of forgiveness that needed time to take root and blossom.

Forgiveness did not come through an apology. Forgiveness was not ushered in by a reconciled relationship. I'm sure that my offender still thinks her attack on me was justified. But in that place where the hurt stuck to me and I staved off forgiveness, God met me, stayed with me, and sustained me.

Romans 5:3–4 says, "We can rejoice, too, when we run into problems and trials, for we know that they help us develop endurance. And endurance develops strength of character, and character strengthens our confident hope of salvation" (NLT). We live in an imperfect world where it's inevitable that we will get hurt. Like you, I certainly do not welcome the pain. But I know that even though I am going to encounter people who, whether intentionally or unintentionally, will hurt me, I can trust God with my heart. Our patient, compassionate, committed, consistent God will hold my assaulted and bruised heart in His hands and nurture me until I feel whole again.

You can trust Him with your heart too.

Questions to Sit With

Ask Yourself

1. What wounds from my past am I allowing to still fester in my heart?
2. Who do I need to forgive today?
3. How has God met me on my long road of pain and brokenness?

Ask God

1. How do You see the person who wronged me?
2. What do You want to teach me or show me through my journey to forgive?
3. Show me my unattended wounds that need time with You.

6

From Heartbreak to Grace

Patricia Raybon

W e're in the kitchen and not talking about Muslims. Instead, my Muslim daughter and I are making pies. Pumpkin. Apple. Crusts just right. Filling on point.

This is the Thanksgiving my daughter wanted. No arguing. No debating. No theological fighting. Just cooking, family, and togetherness. "Look, Mom. We're *bonding*," she says, and we look at each other and laugh. Together.

Both of us know we shouldn't be here. Together? I shouldn't even imagine it.

But God.

I want to say those two words so badly—to start preaching "up in here," as my beautiful urban pastor would say. Instead, I stand in my daughter's Nashville kitchen, measuring out flour, cracking eggs, politely sprinkling nutmeg in the pumpkin pie filling, keeping myself from jabbering about terrorists and mass shootings and my precious daughter's wild, worrisome, and theologically unwieldy journey to Islam.

Our Christian daughter is now a Muslim. And I can find grace in that?

Grace is the last thing I expected in 2001 when she walked away from Jesus, leaving the cross for the crescent. In our long-standing and immovable Christian family, her announcement kicked me to my knees—the best place for a believer, but still the toughest.

As a mother and daughter, our faith battle was "royale," and we fought it hard and ugly. For ten long years we could barely speak to each other without arguing. As poet Adrienne Rich writes, "Probably there is nothing in human nature more resonant with charges than the flow of energy between two biologically alike bodies, one of which has lain in amniotic bliss inside the other, one of which has labored to give birth to the other. The materials are here for the deepest mutuality and the most painful estrangement."[1]

Indeed, I was furious with my daughter's decision. I was embarrassed. I didn't see it coming—this global shift in our family's faith dynamic. We were, after all, determined Sunday churchgoers, and we were real satisfied about it.

As we went to church every Sunday just as I had been raised, my husband and I were passionate and oblivious. We loved how that 7:45 a.m. worship service got us in and out of church fast so that we could get on with our day and our lives.

So, that's what we did. With our youngest daughter in particular, our weeks were full and hectic. She was a busy, pretty teenager: a cheerleader at her high school, a competitive skater on a respected Denver precision ice-skating team,

1. Adrienne Rich, *Of Woman Born: Motherhood as Experience and Institution* (New York: Norton, 2021), 229.

a bit rebellious—although she still dislikes it when I say that. With that "separating from your parents" thing in full swing, Sunday church services were her rare weekly time with family.

It all confused me, for sure. I thought going to church on Sundays—which even she seemed to enjoy—meant being in Christ. Moreover, our African American church experience was high-energy and Christcentric. The music and preaching, as well as the discussion-rich Bible studies and the after-church suppers, made for a deep blend of faith, fun, and fellowship.

But was it really all about Jesus? I thought so.

Later on in her teen years, however, my daughter started saying no. "No, I don't want to go to church this Sunday." "No, I don't understand prayer." "No, God doesn't hear me, so stop talking to me about it all the livelong day. *Please.*"

So, I shut up. I didn't argue for Christ. I didn't invite her to rediscover the Lord. I just assumed she knew Him. Then I sent her off to a prestigious college to face her new life not with Him but alone.

While away at college, she left the family faith altogether. Still hungry to know a god, as she tells it today, she gravitated to students from the Middle East who espoused a belief called Islam. Intrigued by her new friends' modest garb, cultural theology, and claims of a deity "who doesn't need partners"—a reference to Jesus, as she explains it—she left Him for them.

Without warning, she donned a *hijab*, recited Islam's short *Shahada* (profession of faith), and converted.

I got the phone call not long before the 9/11 attacks.

"Hi, Mom. I just called to tell you that I'm a Muslim."

"A what?"

"A Muslim."

And there we were. That long road of walking casually with Christ as a family, of watching a daughter pull away but not knowing how to address her emotional departure, of seeing that she didn't know the Lord for herself but not making it a priority to learn how to fight that particular problem through prayer, had led us to this moment.

"Mom, I'm a Muslim."

Come Sit with Me and Learn Together

For years I told our story with pain and regret. Remorse and heartbreak almost trapped me in an unyielding state of self-condemnation and guilt: *I'm a bad mother. I'm a bad Christian. I'm worth nothing to the kingdom of God, so I should just stop trying to be worth anything to anyone.*

But God.

Remember those words?

They show up in the Bible in the most unlikely places: with rain-soaked Noah (Gen. 8:1); with life-exasperated Jacob (Gen. 31:42); with sibling-challenged Joseph (Gen. 50:20). Standing before his starving, cheating, double-dealing brothers, Joseph invokes the two most grace-soaked words of the Bible: "You intended to harm me, *but God . . .*"

The apostle Paul, writing to the contentious young church in Rome, summarizes it this way: "But God demonstrates his own love for us in this: While we were still sinners, Christ died for us" (Rom. 5:8).

So, I reasoned that if every "but God" in the Bible is true, it had to be true in my relationship with my daughter too.

I had to extend grace to her first. Gritting my teeth some-times—as she would say now, laughing—I stopped battling over religion and granted her the grace of trusting God with the end of our story.

Humbling, indeed, is any family's grace journey.

"Growth in grace," said evangelist Arthur W. Pink, "is a growth *downward*; it is the forming of a lower estimate of ourselves; it is a deepening realization of our nothingness; it is a heartfelt recognition that we are not worthy of the least of God's mercies."[2]

If that is true (and it is), I can decide to cut my daughter some gracious slack. For example, she loathes questions about Islamic terrorists, because she hates feeling like she needs to defend what she insists isn't her true faith. I can be desperate, in contrast, to push her on it—hoping in the ornery places of my heart to score a point for Christ and against her choice of Islam.

But God.

Grace rises to become the best possible gift to offer a loved one, trusting God with the final say, especially when the two of you don't see eye to eye. I learned that the hard way. Beating myself up for failing, I received from the Lord not condemnation but an assuring and welcome break: "Yes, you are a good mother. Yes, you are a good Christian. Yes, you are worth much to My kingdom and to this world, no matter what you or your daughter did or didn't do. So stop sorrowing and get to work. *I need you in the vineyard.*"

This is grace undeserved, as our theologians say.

2. A. W. Pink, *Spiritual Growth: Growth in Grace, or Christian Progress* (Grand Rapids: Baker Book House, 1971), 63, emphasis in original.

Stunned by this grace, I therefore extend it to my daughter. I no longer fight with her. We make our Thanksgiving pies on this Nashville day and never once argue. Instead, I luxuriate in my daughter's kitchen love, watching this woman I raised cook and stir and busy herself in that way that looks like me—even if when we pray we're not yet on the same bright path.

I could berate myself all day, moping around the kitchen and feeling sorrowful about our interfaith dilemma. Instead, I choose to let my daughter love me, to let my grandchildren spoil me, to let my husband joke with me, and to let God assure me. In that way I take grace one step deeper: I extend it to myself.

Scottish preacher Alexander Whyte said, "Grace has only one direction that it can take. Grace always flows down."[3] So, on my knees, I now pray with hope and accept God's love on purpose. This lets me walk, live, and serve without looking back.

Do I regret my motherly mistakes? Decry my parental errors? I could gorge myself on regret until I'm stuffed. Instead, by grace, I eat pie. "Taste and see," says the psalmist, "that the LORD is good" (Ps. 34:8). He is. Always.

---

3. Alexander Whyte, *The Apostle Paul* (Edinburgh: Oliphant Anderson and Ferrier, 1903), 211.

Questions to Sit With

Ask Yourself

1. Who do I want to argue with for Christ who I could instead simply love for Christ?
2. What past mistakes or relationships in my life do I believe are out of God's reach?
3. What would it look like for me to extend grace to myself and others today?

Ask God

1. Jesus, where have I missed You because I made my activities or religion about something else?
2. God, how do You want me to understand or experience the gift of Your grace in a deeper way?
3. Lord, show me how to love and let grace flow down to the person whose choices disappoint me or whose beliefs I'll never be on the same page with.

7

Staying Friends When You Share More Differences Than Similarities

Kristen Strong

The high desert sun beat down heavy on my friend and me as we wrestled our six kiddos into my minivan. This longtime gal pal, Yvonne, and her three young girls were visiting our small house from out of state. And while the kids all got along well, with only the occasional argument over Lincoln Logs or Legos, we two moms could be a different story. Or at least it felt like a different story. And on that July afternoon, the sun wasn't the only thing that burned hot.

My anger did as well.

Before we all climbed into the car, my friend and I had argued over a hot-button topic that we saw from completely different sides. I went into that exchange mighty frustrated because I'd already endured a barrage of criticisms from her. For example, the mattress in the spare bedroom was uneven and uncomfortable, and my breakfast options weren't healthy and nutritious.

I took it all in stride, pausing for a lot of deep breaths—that is, until the triple-digit temperatures and my exhaustion and crankiness made my own temperature shoot upward. When Yvonne went looking to spar over a controversial issue, I was happy to oblige. That exchange ended abruptly when I was midsentence in defending my viewpoint and Yvonne rolled her eyes at me, waved her hand dismissively in the air, and did a complete one-eighty before leaving the room altogether.

If I think about it for too long, the rejection bound up in that dismissive gesture still stings. I wasn't some stranger whose opinion she'd come across online. I was a flesh-and-blood friend she'd known since college. How could she be so dismissive as to shrug me off like that?

From my point of view, Yvonne seemed blind to my hospitality and singularly focused on pointing out all my shortcomings and faulty reasonings.

From Yvonne's point of view, I was the annoying, small-minded Christian who had all the answers and saw the world in black and white. And she wasn't necessarily wrong. In many ways, I truly did think I knew better. I thought that an unvocalized opinion was an invalid one. If someone like Yvonne put me on the defensive, I often made the poor choice of reacting in a way that only threw gasoline on the fire.

To further complicate things, Yvonne was not a Christian, and I worried long and hard about her salvation. Every so often I would clumsily open the door on faith issues, and she would definitively slam it shut.

On that hot afternoon inside the minivan, I gripped the steering wheel like I was maneuvering big-city traffic. I asked myself, *Why do our get-togethers dissolve more and more into uncomfortable disagreements?* Yes, Yvonne and I lived on different sides of the country, and this made it difficult to regularly see each other in the first place. But we also lived on different sides of several issues, and that made it difficult to willingly listen to each other's point of view.

Looking back on it today, I realize a shift occurred during that particular get-together. For the majority of our lives, each of us had traveled in the same direction in close relationship. But that visit served as a counterweight of sorts that knocked into both of us. Instead of intersecting as we'd done for years through similar interests, opinions, and ideas, we began traveling in different directions altogether. The ever-growing gap of our differences began to overshadow our similarities.

I suppose we could've stayed stuck in that cavernous gap, even shrugging our shoulders in resignation that our friendship wasn't worth the effort it would take to not irritate the living daylights out of each other. I'm grateful to say we made a different choice.

Following that particular visit, Yvonne and I began interacting with each other differently. Time, and I suppose more than a little maturity, helped us see there was a better way to engage. I don't remember either of us directly addressing our changed relationship, although we each apologized for how we handled things on that fateful visit. But shortly afterwards, we each seemed to understand we had a choice: either we could continue to insist we were right about all the things or we could have a relationship. We couldn't have both.

In my own heart, I realized that Jesus put a high priority on relationships with people He differed from, and I needed to do a better job of following His lead.

In the years since that visit, Yvonne and I have seen each other a handful of times, but we text regularly and stay in touch. We talk about the similarities we do have—our alma mater, our profession, and our shared love for a good chai latte. There's been a more easygoing nature to our time together as I do my best to reach for grace rather than react and as she compliments rather than criticizes.

And we both have learned that judiciously keeping an opinion to ourselves doesn't invalidate it. It only helps us to listen sensibly . . . and to love lavishly.

Come Sit with Me and Learn Together

After that contentious visit fifteen years ago, I never would have thought that the arrows of our lives could move toward each other again. But in His grace, God can always orchestrate a turnaround.

Now, I should mention that I've been in other friendships or relationships that have taken such a toxic turn that boundaries needed to be erected. I've never locked a door between myself and someone else, but I have shut it with instructions that it would not be reopened unless the other person's style of communication changed. In the words of Jennifer Dukes Lee, "You can set limits and be a loving person at the same time."[1] Knowing when to move forward with or without

1. Jennifer Dukes Lee, *Growing Slow* (Grand Rapids: Zondervan, 2021), 106.

boundaries in a relationship takes wisdom, discernment, and the Holy Spirit's guidance. But whatever direction you go, I believe this foundational truth ought to be carried along the way: *we must love people where they are, not where we wish they were.* Part of having a hospitable spirit is accepting this through and through.

Once Yvonne and I figured this out, we were free to enjoy a friendship based on love and respect, not shared opinions and ideology. We were able to love each other by accepting where the other person was, even if it wasn't where we thought the other "should" be.

Since I can only control what I think, say, and do, I realized I did not have the power to say or do anything to open Yvonne's heart to the Lord. This truth is reflected in Scripture. When the Israelites were exiled to Babylon because they had sinned by turning away from the Lord, God gave His people a powerful reminder that He is the one who softens hardened hearts: "And I will give you a new heart, and a new spirit I will put within you. And I will remove the heart of stone from your flesh and give you a heart of flesh" (Ezek. 36:26 ESV).

I've not addressed issues of faith again with Yvonne, except as it naturally comes up in conversation related to what's going on in my day-to-day life. All my talking and cajoling won't transform Yvonne's heart. Transformative heart work must be done from the inside out, and only God can do that. Jesus's saving work on the cross is the singular action that not only covers our shortcomings and sins but also paves the way for a heart to change.

It takes two people to make a friendship work, and I can only work on my own heart with the help of the Holy Spirit.

However, I can pray for the other person's heart—and let go of everything else.

Yvonne and I may still differ in our worldviews and on some of today's hot-button topics. But whether we catch up via text or in person, we listen and encourage. We agree on being *for* each other moment by moment, day by day.

And that's something I hope we always, *always* agree on.

Questions to Sit With

Ask Yourself

1. Is there a friend or family member with whom I have more differences than similarities, yet I still feel called to be in relationship with him or her?
2. When I examine my own heart, is there a defensive streak or something that makes it hard to listen more and talk less?
3. What are some benefits of maintaining relationships with others who are very different from me?

Ask God

1. Lord, Your Word tells me "in humility consider others as more important than yourselves"[2]—no caveats. Show me when I start to believe I'm better than others. What traces of pride do You want to remove from my heart?

2. Phil. 2:3 CSB.

2. What does it look like to grow a hospitable spirit with all those You place in my circle of influence, not just those with whom I share more similarities than differences?
3. Father in heaven, in what relationships am I failing to accept someone as they are?

8

Standing Ovations and Longing to Be Loved

Anjuli Paschall

Tucked away among winding hillsides and sporadic homes is a winery where I sat with my dearest people. The restaurant was on the edge of the earth. I let out a sigh, grateful for this rare evening when I got to sip sangria, tear clumps of salty bread, and be with my husband, sister, and brother-in-law—a double date with family members who are also beloved friends. We paused. We held one another in a sacred gaze, and we were held by the expansive beauty swooping under and all around us. For the past several years, my sister and her family have lived overseas, making moments like this one abundantly special.

With the sun still ablaze, we casually sipped our drinks and scanned the sloping hillside. As we looked over a valley of patchwork fields and farms, we let our eyes ease our souls into the peace we had all been craving. Without formality, we passed around curious questions for one another like we passed the single menu. Safe people are easy to be with. There isn't a temptation to fill in the silence with sarcasm or to analyze pop culture. Instead, one by one, we shared our stories. Stories from adventures abroad. Stories of stress that toppled us over into a storm of tears. Stories about loneliness in a foreign world. Sitting together and nibbling on slender crackers slathered with blue cheese, we listened to each other share pain, wrestle with the unknown, and acknowledge the life regrets we still carry on our backs.

A question was gently lobbed to me: "What is it like to move into this next season with your kids all in school?" How could I sum up my life's drastic shift in a few coherent sentences? I rambled on and on about my youngest starting preschool and my oldest hurling his football bag over his shoulder as I watched him walk through the gates of his high school. I talked about losing a few things but gaining so much more. I told them how I cried after school drop-off, not because I was sad but, oddly, because I was proud.

The last fifteen years have been hard. Growing babies, weaning babies, changing babies, disciplining toddlers, managing schedules, and years without sleep have been, in one word, challenging. It was extremely exhausting, but I didn't give up. Looking back, I realized I was there for the post-nap snuggles, lightning-speed questions, and barrage of daily demands. I was there for the morning tea parties and afternoon forts. I was there. I did it. I got my kids to school alive and (mostly) dressed appropriately. I was proud of myself, I shared.

Then, one by one, my precious crew started clapping for me. For some people this might be the moment they turn inward, blushing with embarrassment. But me, I teared up with joy and sat up a little straighter with pride. Even at that moment, I knew this accomplishment wasn't mine alone. It was the work of God in me. Who I was fifteen years ago is so different from who I am today. God raised me as I raised my children.

Sometimes we forget to celebrate with one another. We forget to stop and say, "I'm proud of you" or "Well done." But there in the middle of the restaurant, my favorite people gave me a standing ovation. With other diners staring and smiling in our direction, I couldn't help but feel grateful for the ways God changed me, helped me, and grew me. I didn't stand and take a bow, but I did cry and laugh a little too.

We don't stop and cheer one another on often enough. We are quick to move into the next season without acknowledging what God has done in the past. It's so meaningful to be with others in their joy—and to vulnerably invite others into ours. It's important to stop, look around, and take in the masterpiece God has painted in the world and in one another.

As the evening came to a close, we snapped a few photos against the majestic backdrop of vine-covered hills. I let my soul soak in the creamy light floating just above the landscape. My heart was fully alive and abundantly content. Remembering God's goodness, giving thanks for His faithfulness, and enjoying the friendships around me made my heart clap. As I savored this moment, hope welled up inside my chest. Looking out into eternity, I was wordless. I let my heart stand in awe and marveled at what God had done in me. I think this was my standing ovation for God's work in my life. When God does incredible things in our lives and the lives of others, how can we not holler in praise or let the holy miracle move us into silent awe?

Come Sit with Me and Learn Together

For most people it's easy to come together on straightforward issues. We can stand around the appetizer table and talk about the best movies or who recently had a baby. We can agree on how fabulous the new Thai restaurant is or on the next book to read for our book club. Coming together on challenging topics is a stretch. We would rather have the harder conversations through our screens so we don't have to make eye contact and can pretend we never butted heads online when we run into each other in the frozen foods aisle. It's like avoiding conflict and discomfort is coded into our DNA.

But I never realized how hard it is to be with others in their joy. Oftentimes another person's joy can seemingly diminish our own. Like when a friend gets a huge job promotion and now your tiny raise seems inconsequential. Or you're fighting for peace and growth in your marriage and someone gushes about how great their spouse is and how easy their marriage is, and suddenly you feel like you're losing the battle. Somehow we make life a competition. Because of this, it's challenging not only to genuinely celebrate with others in their joy but also to allow others to see and celebrate what delights our heart. Sharing my feeling of pride about raising my children meant being vulnerable. Perhaps gathering in any meaningful way requires vulnerability.

Sitting beside people in their pain and in their accomplishments becomes a place where we have to face our own pain and evaluate our own accomplishments (or lack thereof). To show up for others in love requires that we also show up with full awareness of ourselves. We have to experience our sin, shortcomings, and pain. This means our hearts will inevitably feel weak, inadequate, and without words. It takes courage to step out of what feels safe and be with others no matter where they are.

Thankfully, we don't step into the unknown alone. We are led by Jesus, who welcomes all of His children to the table. It takes being vulnerable, but there is no other way to love and be loved than to pull out a chair with Jesus and listen to others' stories, ask them questions, and be curious about the journeys they are on. Grab a tissue, pour another glass of water, turn off your phone, make direct eye contact, clap when necessary. Under their stories is a deeper one—a story about a human who just longs to be loved.

Questions to Sit With

Ask Yourself

1. Do I find it easy or challenging to be with others in their joy?
2. Who is someone in my life right now that I can sit with in their accomplishments?
3. When has someone celebrated me? How did that make me feel?

Ask God

1. God, how can I grow as a person who stands up and claps for others?
2. God, search my heart and reveal my sin to me. How and why have I resisted celebrating others?
3. God, how do You sit with me in my joy?

9

When You Feel Alone in the Struggle

Kathi Lipp

I've never thought of myself as an "us versus them" kind of girl. I'm the person who tried never to exclude people at the fourth-grade lunch table because I just so badly wanted to be included. Making sure everyone belonged, every time, was a badge I wore as proudly as the ones I stapled onto my Girl Scout sash in elementary school. (I obviously never earned my sewing badge.)

One of the ways I have been most proud of including people is in my stories that deal with being overweight. If you love me, you might call me "curvy" or "Rubenesque." But if you're on the internet, hidden by a computer screen, you might call me "huge" or "gross." I've been called both. By Christians. In God's love, of course. Because, as I've been reminded over and over again, "gluttony is a sin."

So I wrote an article for all my curvy friends who struggle with their weight. I wrote to say that while you may not always love your body size, God can use it, because others who see your struggle can know that you are a safe person compared to those who appear perfect.

And I heard from women. A lot of women.

It felt great to give a voice to these women who so often feel like the world is not built for them. I heard from a lot of people who said, "This is exactly my story" or "I feel this so deeply." So many of us have the same story. Because of our appearance, we've felt judged before fully stepping into the room. We've felt excluded when people critique our perceived weakness before we've even had a conversation with them. We've felt like "less than" Christians because of our battle with our weight.

But now we curvy girls had found each other, and we could see each other in our shared imperfection. The presumption was, "You are safe and you are loved exactly as you are." I was excited to know that women who often feel so "other" were finding a measure of hope and peace through my words. Talking about my weight is never easy, but I'm willing to do it so that someone else can feel more seen and less alone.

Can I be honest with you? I even wanted to start a club for Christian women whose BMI is not socially acceptable. I wanted a permanent safe place where we could build a fort and not let any of those mean voices from our everyday lives (or, even worse, the internet) have the password to get in. I had found my people, and we shopped in the plus-size section.

So, I was a little taken aback by the voice message I got from my newish friend, Becky Keife, who started out by saying, "I just need you to know what an impact your article has had on me." She went on to say that she had never before thought of her weakness as being a shortcut to connection, and she was grateful to have this new perspective, all because I'd been vulnerable in an article.

Why did I find this odd? Because one look at Becky would confirm that she is not and probably never has been plus-sized. I had to take a beat. Why would she connect with my article about being fat?

And to be perfectly honest, for just a moment I thought, "But I didn't write this article for you."

It never occurred to me that someone who didn't look like me could understand or connect with my experience. I was so busy trying to connect with the people who looked like me that I became the one "othering" someone who felt the same pangs of struggle I did, just with a lower BMI.

You see, what I didn't know about Becky is that she suffers from clinical anxiety. And my article talked about weakness being a shortcut to trust. My weakness? My weight. Becky's weakness? Her anxiety.

I guess in my own myopic view I thought that someone like Becky couldn't understand what it felt like to be outside the scope of socially "normal." But there she was, in a struggle different from but in many ways so much like my own.

Come Sit with Me and Learn Together

It is small and shortsighted of me to assume that a person is not suffering on the inside just because they look like the world's version of perfect on the outside. Or that they can't be used by God in the same way I can because their challenges aren't as visible as mine.

I know all of this on paper. I just get it mixed up in my mind. And my heart.

I confessed all of this to Becky. My assumptions about her seemingly perfect life without the struggle of weight. The idea that she couldn't relate to me because we hadn't worn the same size jeans. I'm so glad I was wrong. Becky may not be in my BMI club, but she showed me that the circle of vulnerability and struggle is much wider than I thought. Showing up with our stories and a healing dose of love and grace was the invitation we both needed to enter into each other's circles.

Later, Becky texted me this one simple sentence: "Assumptions are barriers to connection, but stories are bridges to understanding."

Exactly.

While each of us can feel isolated by our differences, the core feelings we experience in those differences are universal. When I am singled out for being overweight, I feel judged, abandoned, and unloved. And someone who has a different struggle from mine will experience those same feelings. When we're brave to share our stories, anyone can apply the lessons we've learned:

- God shows His strength in our struggles.
- Our struggles can be a shortcut to connection.
- God uses broken people in powerful ways.
- While our struggles are different, our God loves to lift each of us.

I built barriers by making assumptions about others. Now I need to listen to the stories of those whose battles are different from mine and start building bridges of under-standing.

I've spent years trying to get rid of the prejudices in my own heart. But one thing I have learned is that I don't know what I don't know. If I've never been brave enough to ask God to search my heart and root out any falsehoods that have taken up residence there, how will I know how much further I have to go?

I've read Psalm 26:2 a thousand times, but recently I've had to work up the courage to actually pray this prayer: "Test me, LORD, and try me, examine my heart and my mind." It seems so simple, but it is a brave prayer, and its impact could be life changing. I don't know about you, but I feel like it's one of the scariest prayers a person can pray.

Asking God to test me?

Asking God to try me?

Asking God to examine my heart?

Asking God to examine my mind?

I continue to pray this prayer regularly, and it continues to change me. And that change is hard. Because when you've felt for years like the maligned person, it's hard to share space with someone who seemingly doesn't struggle in the same way.

And can I tell you, that is a whole different kind of uncom-fortable than not being invited to sit at the cool kids' table.

That, my friend, is heart and head uncomfortable. But comfort and change are not compatible. We have to be will-ing to sit in a space of discomfort in order to open our-selves up to the kind of heart change that can transform our relationships—with God and with others. And that kind of change is worth it.

Questions to Sit With

Ask Yourself

1. What is one thing I struggle with that makes me feel disconnected from others who don't share that struggle?
2. Which groups of "other" people do I hold assumptions about that are probably false?
3. Are there any obstacles keeping me from asking God to examine my heart and mind? If so, what are they?

Ask God

1. Lord, when have I unwittingly excluded people because of my incorrect perceptions?
2. Which relationships do You want me to foster by forging new connections?
3. In what ways do I need to give up my comfort in order to change?

10

How to Deal with Toxic People

Bonnie Gray

Michelle was a friend from high school. She was always nice to me, sharing her lunch and inviting me to her house after school to study. While we had a great friendship as teenagers, the dynamics changed once we grew up and became moms. Whenever I'd mention feeling overwhelmed with motherhood, like how the laundry was piling up, she'd make comments like, "That's because you *let* laundry pile up. You wait until the weekend when it's a big pile and it becomes a big chore. I do my laundry in small loads throughout the week. If you did that, your kids wouldn't have to hunt for socks in the morning."

I was surprised my friend even remembered my chaotic sock incident from a few weeks earlier. I laughed it off in a self-effacing manner and scolded myself. *Stop being so sensitive. She's just being helpful.*

But our phone calls left me feeling less-than. Our conversations came to focus more on how I could be doing something better, and she'd end up giving me unsolicited advice. I felt increasing stress each time we talked, but I didn't know what to say. I was afraid of conflict. I was afraid of losing her friendship.

A similar thing started happening in my relationship with Laura, a ministry leader I served alongside. She'd been complimentary of my leadership and even initiated having coffee together so she could "mentor" me. I felt grateful someone wanted to invest time into me. Our get-togethers started out encouraging. But over time Laura began making judgments that left me feeling confused and unsure of myself. She'd say things like, "I think you may not be trusting God in this" and "You're not standing in the truth!" Even though I didn't agree with her, she was very authoritative and I didn't know how to disagree. I wanted to be gracious.

Because Laura and I were serving together, I wanted to keep the peace. I didn't want to accuse her of being judgmental. But how do you extricate yourself from someone who makes you feel unduly guilty and yet is in a position of influence?

In both of these situations, I asked God to change these women and to change me. *Lord, help me to stop feeling bad about myself and to have more grace.* But no matter how hard I prayed, I still felt increasingly anxious in these relationships.

What I didn't realize at the time is that these people were emotionally toxic. If their comments were taken out of context, nothing they said appeared glaringly wrong or inaccurate or abusive. But I found myself filled with anxiety after each interaction with them.

Over time, I learned that one cause of anxiety and depression is hiding how we feel for fear of being rejected or gaslighted. Gaslighting happens when someone manipulates you into questioning your reality or invalidates your experiences, views, or feelings as being wrong, too sensitive, or imagined. God wasn't answering my prayers to change these women or to change how I was feeling because God wanted me to face the truth: these relationships were toxic to my well-being.

I needed to change my boundaries. I needed to learn to speak up and have a voice. I needed to prioritize my well-being so I could be free to experience the peace and joy God intends for each of us as His beloved children.

Each time I pushed away my feelings because I was afraid of conflict, afraid of disapproval, or afraid of losing a friendship, I became invisible. I was not living by faith. I was living in fear.

Jesus says, "Come to me, all of you who are weary and burdened, and I will give you rest" (Matt. 11:28 CSB). I began to read that Scripture passage in a new light and apply it to the toxic and dysfunctional relationships in my life. I was exhausted from the weight of feeling responsible for other people's negative feelings. I heard Jesus gently asking, "What if you stopped carrying the burden of making sure no one is upset with you?"

Nothing made me more uncomfortable than the idea of someone being upset with me, disappointed in me, or disapproving of me. But the gentle voice of the Shepherd whispered that He cared more about my emotional and spiritual wellness than my comfort. He cared more about my freedom than my maintaining appearances for the sake of a toxic friendship.

So I began to ask myself two questions. If I am being uncomfortably honest, (1) What relationship in my life is toxic and why? (2) What do I need to say or do to move that relationship toward a healthier place?

Lord, help me to be more honest than I am comfortable with. This was a prayer God placed on my heart. And it did not go away until I acted on it.

Come Sit with Me and Learn Together

Asking these questions led me on a life-changing journey to reevaluate the coping mechanisms I had developed over the years. To survive growing up in a dysfunctional family, I internalized every abusive word and took on the role of caretaker and peacemaker, no matter the personal cost. I believed it was up to me to make sure everyone was okay. This was my duty.

But God was on a quest to dismantle my own toxic beliefs and the coping mechanisms that no longer protected me. God was now empowering me to grow in my faith and to heal in ways I never knew were possible.

God never meant for us to carry the burden of changing other people's minds about us. He never meant for us to be responsible for other people's emotional baggage, sin, and wounds.

I had to learn to create healthy boundaries, and I had to ask God for courage to speak the truth to the toxic people in my life. This wasn't easy for me. Maybe it's not easy for you either. My father left when I was seven. I didn't have an earthly, loving father who gave me permission to be honest. My mother was not a loving person. She was verbally and emotionally abusive, always making me question my choices and putting me in a double bind. It was always either her way or the highway. My mother's way of controlling me was to make me feel guilty, so that in order to prove my love to her, I had to do X, Y, and Z.

But I have a loving heavenly Father who is rewriting those scripts. Because of Jesus, I don't have to stay stuck in the painful and destructive patterns of my past. Jesus welcomes us just as we are. He loves us unconditionally, whether we are happy or angry, sad or cheerful, worried or carefree. Jesus meets us where we are and invites us to a new life in Him.

On my healing journey, I recognized all the ways I repeated the long-ingrained, unhealthy pattern of trying to appease toxic people. I incorrectly believed that if only I could love them and care for them more or be kinder to them, *then* they would stop being toxic. But toxic people exploit the desire to keep the peace and the fear of rejection. You can't change another person, but you can learn healthy ways to handle hard relationships.

Here are five tips for coping with toxic people:

1. *Don't stay silent. You matter. Tell someone about the toxic person in your life.*

   It is not your job to protect the toxic person who has hurt you. You need to protect yourself. You are worthy to be loved. The first step to protecting yourself is to speak the truth. You've tried with all your might to protect that person who is wounding or has wounded you. But suffering in silence is not what our loving Savior wants for you.

   As I write books, speak to women, and share my story of breaking free from toxic relationships to

be God's beloved daughter, I am often asked, "But
if I speak up about my [fill in the blank: mom, dad,
husband, children, pastor, church leader, girlfriend,
mommy-friend, ex-boyfriend, ex-spouse], won't it
reflect badly on them? I don't know how to share
without making them look bad." It's normal to have
a fear of shame and to not want others to think you
have a bad marriage, bad children, bad ministry, bad
family, and so on.

In response, I say, "I care about *you*. Jesus cares
about *you*! He cares about your well-being. God does
not want you to hurt anymore. You are God's beloved daughter!"

2. *Create boundaries. Even if you feel guilty, it does not
mean you are guilty.*

The toxic person wants to exert control over the
narrative of your relationship and life through their
words or behavior. When you create boundaries, they
will become upset and say things to make you feel
guilty in order to keep you within the box of your
fears, inaction, and silence.

Just because a toxic person accuses you of being
uncaring, overly sensitive, or selfish does not make
it true. You do not need to justify your boundaries.
You have freedom to set boundaries to protect your
well-being.

3. *Enlist support and role-play conversations.*

Being assertive and speaking up for yourself with
a toxic person is a new, odd, and scary experience if

you've never been given permission to do so. Not sure
what to say or where to start? That's okay. Don't be
shy to ask a loving friend to help you write a script
and role-play the boundaries conversation with you.
We all need practice and support in creating new patterns of relating. That's what I had to do.

4. *Limit the time you spend with toxic people.*

People who are emotionally toxic are very good
at intimidation, manipulation, and gaslighting, so
be gentle with yourself. It is easy to feel confused,
anxious, and scared, or to freeze up when you engage
with a toxic person, so limit the time you spend with
them.

When conversations get overwhelming, stick to
stating what they did or said, how it makes you feel,
and what action you will take and the changes you
will make. Do not ask the toxic person for permission to enact these changes. You are not seeking
agreement. You are communicating your boundaries.

5. *Grieve the death of expectations and dreams.*

I had to grieve the death of my expectations and
dreams for the ideal friend, mentor, and mom I
longed for so I could grow into the daughter of a
loving heavenly Father. Jesus said, "You will know
the truth, and the truth will set you free" (John 8:32
CSB). It's important to God that we trust Him with
the truth, even if it hurts. We experience a powerful
rest when we give God the burdens we were never
meant to carry.

People sometimes ask me if I've forgiven my mother for the decades of verbal and emotional abuse. I have done the hard work of grieving and healing. I have forgiven my mother. She was my whole life, and I love her more than anyone may understand.

While forgiveness takes one person, reconciliation takes two. Loving our parent, spouse, friend, mentor, or pastor does not mean open borders to toxicity, fear, intimidation, or manipulation.

We can begin to make different choices that are healthy for ourselves and that break old, hurtful patterns. We can stop being enablers for hurtful people in our lives so that they, too, can face the truth of their brokenness with God.

Questions to Sit With

Ask Yourself

1. Who are the toxic people in my life, and why is it so hard to prioritize my own well-being?
2. If I was being more honest than I am comfortable with, what would I say about the toxic people in my life?
3. What expectations of an ideal relationship do I need to grieve and face the truth about?

Ask God

1. What is the truth You want me to acknowledge, confront, and embrace?

2. What coping mechanisms do You want me to surrender, and what boundaries do You want me to create?

3. Show me what I am afraid of in these toxic relationships and how You want to free me to live differently.

11

The Unexpected Gift of an Age Gap

Melissa Zaldivar

I had a plan. I was seventeen years old and getting ready to graduate high school, and I had dreams of leaving my small California town, playing golf, and majoring in music. I'd visited a dreamy campus where I auditioned for the music department and had been awarded a scholarship. I bought the sweatshirt. I knew that my future was there.

But then life happened. College is expensive, and attending my dream school just wasn't possible. It was a private school in Southern California, and the scholarships weren't enough. I clung to some kind of false sense of hope that maybe my parents would win the lottery and told everyone I was going there, but as the enrollment deadline approached, I filled out a registration form at my local community college.

As my friends went off to the far corners of the world, posting photos to the very new platform called Facebook, I felt left behind. I was stuck in my small town, commuting to campus a few days a week and working in a local bookstore.

I thought that my college days would be filled with new faces and new experiences, but everything around me was familiar. Life felt like a weird sequel, one in which the plot didn't change much from the original movie. After all the hype, I honestly felt a little embarrassed. Sheepishly, I dreamed of getting the heck out of that place while trying my best to accept it for what it was.

I kept attending the same church I'd grown up in my entire life, and one day a woman named Debbie approached me to ask if I'd like to join her and some other ladies for a Tuesday night Bible study. These women were not the demographic I'd expected to spend time with. At least half of them had changed my diapers when I was a baby and were now starting to retire and consider the best ways to engage with their grandkids. On the outside it didn't look like we had much in common. But by the grace of God, I agreed to join them.

At first I felt a little uncomfortable because my life seemed very small and my problems probably made them laugh. I was wrestling through singleness and homework and trying to find my place in the world, which seemed like a far cry from the season of life they were in. But week after week these women welcomed me to join them at Debbie's little farmhouse. They let me eat homemade snacks (which everyone brought at some point, but I never seemed to be on the rotation) and they listened to the prayer requests of an eighteen-year-old. In retrospect, I cringe a bit when I think about the things that used to concern me most. Bless them.

I don't remember a whole lot of what I learned in the classroom that first year of college. In fact, I think only two classes ended up transferring to the school I attended the rest of my undergrad career. But I remember sitting in the living room of Debbie's house out in the country and hearing stories of God's faithfulness.

One evening I said, "I know that some of the things I talk about seem trivial."

A kind-faced woman who had known me my whole life smiled and said, "You remind me of the passion that I used to have, and it makes me remember those years so fondly."

I had never considered that maybe I was contributing something. If anything, I assumed I was probably annoying and too young to be able to fully connect. But goodness, I am glad that God proved me wrong.

Come Sit with Me and Learn Together

We live in a day and age when so many of us are separated according to our generation or life season, but Scripture is full of intergenerational relationships. We see the loyalty of Ruth to her mother-in-law, Naomi. We witness Moses encouraging the Israelites to pass down God's law to their children and grandchildren. First Peter 5:5 says, "You who are younger, be subject to the elders" (ESV). And Hebrews 13:7 encourages believers to "remember your leaders, those who spoke to you the word of God. Consider the outcome of their way of life, and imitate their faith" (ESV). Book after book shows the story of the people of God learning to follow Him together.

And the learning and discipleship don't go just one way! No, we're told in 1 Timothy 4:12, "Let no one despise you for your youth, but set the believers an example in speech, in conduct, in love, in faith, in purity" (ESV). A young person setting an example? That seems almost contrary to conventional wisdom. Age is what affords us knowledge and experience, and yet God knows that we all have something to learn from those older *and* younger than us. Recall Jesus's words from Matthew 18:3: "Truly, I say to you, unless you turn and become like children, you will never enter the kingdom of heaven" (ESV). He is actually encouraging us to be childlike when we're grown!

I'd often thought that the pattern of the local church was for us to look more or less the same, but in reality? Our differences are a gift! Think of the richness to be found in different generations and cultures and even denominational preferences. Yes, we come together around big-picture stuff, like the fact that the Bible is really God's Word and Jesus really rose from the grave. But there's still a whole lot of perspective that we miss out on when we try to be spiritual clones.

I once heard someone lament that they wished there were no denominations and we were all exactly the same in our beliefs and practices. And while I understand the sentiment, let me put on my church historian hat for a moment. See, when the church was first established nearly two thousand years ago, they needed clarity about what they believed, so a few generations in, there was a council that met to figure out exactly what Christians believed based on Scripture. They gave us big building blocks that were heavy and took up a lot of space. Perhaps you've heard of the Nicene Creed or the Apostles' Creed. The word *creed* comes from the Latin word *credo*, which literally means "I believe." There were all kinds of people who were taking Christianity and distorting it, so leaders came together to say, "This is where we draw the line. These are the essentials." Now, there are also nonessentials—things that we don't always have clarity about or things that might look different to different people. Some people baptize babies and others baptize adults. Some people disagree about the specific roles of men and women within the church. These are issues that are debated among Christians, but they're not the essentials.

The nonessentials are important, but they're not the main focus or gravitational pull of the foundation of our faith. No one is a heretic for taking communion with grape juice instead of wine. These are preferences, not things that get you kicked out of Christianity. And the reason that there are so many denominations? Historically, the church hasn't always agreed on those nonessentials, so over the centuries and millennia, they decided to go their separate ways. Lutherans and Methodists and Baptists and Presbyterians are all a result of someone saying, "Let's agree to disagree."

And maybe that's why I love the fact that there are so many different denominations under the umbrella of Christianity: we all bring something different to the table, but it's still a feast. We're like a giant potluck of believers. We don't all bring only homemade potato salad or only macaroni and cheese or only Caesar salad we bought in a prepared bag because we forgot until we were halfway through listening to the sermon that there was a potluck after church.

So, back to my adolescent woes. I applied to another school and was accepted for my second year of college. It was in Chicago, so I was moving far away. My transition was made smoother by the notes and care packages my more seasoned California church pals sent. Even after I left their midweek Bible study, these women continued to pour into me. Now, over ten years later, I still go walk with them or join them for Bible study whenever I visit my hometown. Last summer they celebrated twenty-five years of opening God's Word together in that little farmhouse, and it felt sacred to reunite and sing songs and tell stories of how God has moved in each of our lives.

I wouldn't be who I am without those women who have a different perspective from mine. Their wisdom has shaped me and pointed me to Jesus over and over again. The women I thought I'd have nothing in common with became sisters, and it was only possible because God kept me in that little town for my first year of college. Think of all I would have missed out on if I hadn't accepted Debbie's invitation! I wouldn't be as rich in relationships as I am now, that's for sure, and I certainly wouldn't have some very sweet texts on my phone that they still send to let me know they're praying for me.

So, go ahead—sit with someone who wasn't born in your decade or denomination or city. You'll both be better for it—and if you're lucky, they might feed you too.

Questions to Sit With

Ask Yourself

1. Who are some women I could welcome into my circle that are older or younger than I am?
2. How would it change my perspective to hear from women in other seasons of life?
3. What am I afraid of when it comes to opening up to someone different from me?

Ask God

1. God, how can You help me to be brave in trusting others?
2. God, how do You see differences as a good thing?
3. Jesus, what do You mean in Matthew 18:1–5, where You say that we should be like children?

12

Tenderness Is the Only Way Forward

Tasha Jun

Early in the pandemic my kids and I hung origami cranes from our crab apple tree. We chose a variety of colored and flower-patterned papers to fold into birds and then punched a hole at the tips of their tails for the string.

In the midst of a brand-new season of school at home, with vocabulary like "quarantine" and "stay-at-home orders" defining our new reality, with canceled plans and looking at news headlines every hour, something as small as folding origami cranes felt like grace for our eyes and hands.

We watched the pointy birds sway in the wind, all colorful and proud against the backdrop of a bright blue sky, and then the next morning I had to untangle them from the branches and from each other. Overnight their strings had wound so tightly that they were bound. Even the dew at dawn was too much for their fragile paper skins.

Back then, my own tenderness toward others was soft in a fresh sort of way. I wouldn't have believed you if you'd told me just how jostled we'd all become over the next twelve-plus months, or how so many of us would swing into tangles that seemed impossible to free. Just a few months before hanging those birds, I co-led a four-week Bible study series on friendship at our church with one of my closest friends, Sandy. We talked about the unlikely bond between Ruth and Naomi and about how our own friendship had begun without our choosing, and yet it was a source of strength and an obvious gift of God's goodness to each of us. We ended the series on such a high note. It had always been a dream and prayer of ours to work alongside each other and minister to other women together.

The day after the last talk of our series, I went for a morning bike ride on what felt like the most perfect October day. Fifteen minutes into the ride, I fell off my bike and broke my wrist in the worst way. It was my friend Sandy who picked up my boys from school that day and treated them to dinner, then picked up my daughter, who was at the hospital with me. It was Sandy who brought us meals and checked in on me day after day, just like she'd always done.

But at the height of Covid, a week after my kids and I hung our paper birds, we followed a popular new pandemic tradition and put teddy bears in our windows. We ordered drawing pencils, sketchbooks, and activity books, and we walked round and round the neighborhood as a family. I baked cookies and made afternoon Dalgona coffees on repeat. We marveled over the creative ways our community reached out to one another: texting more, downloading new apps like Marco Polo, FaceTiming one another, and celebrating birthdays with signs, drive-bys, porch drop-offs, and video greetings. The grace of God felt near and abundant despite our looming fears back then. It was easy to recognize Jesus in all these acts of love, and I expected them to be enough.

Then summer, then fall, then winter came and went, more months of disappointment, and the magnitude of loss and mounting racial tensions further shook the foundations we stood on. I had no idea that breaking my wrist in the fall of 2019 would be the first in a series of hard things that carried on into 2020. We all know how the collective story goes.

All the impossible decisions around Covid left the deep divides we read about in online articles and impacted some of my life's most grounding relationships. Six months into 2020, after a series of texts about family and needs and struggle, Sandy told me she and her family were going to try another church, and my heart sank—not because of the church but because I knew it would change everything. And it did. Sandy and I didn't lose our friendship, but we lost parts of what it had been, and we lost a common place of community and worship.

I've asked Jesus how we're supposed to move forward after all of this, and He keeps nudging me to tenderness amid the pain.

Come Sit with Me and Learn Together

As I write this, restrictions ease and we begin to reengage, and I feel the impact of what's been lost everywhere—from walking an aisle in Target to gathering with our now-altered small group. Maybe reengaging is still fresh for you too, or maybe you're feeling a long-familiar angst that has scabbed over. Either way, there's no going back to what was. There's only showing up to what is—what's changed, what's broken, and what's still healing.

There is grief I'm still not sure how to approach in the wake of 2020. Cynicism has shown up at my door, looking like the stronger and safer guide forward.

I read through the Gospels, desperate to find the tenderness of Jesus because my own tenderness feels like a stranger. In one instance after another, Jesus's tenderness leads the way. It moves me to read and reread John 4 and to remember how He went to Sychar in Samaria. He intentionally arrives there thirsty and tired. Jesus, the Living Water, humbly asks a woman, a Samaritan, for a drink. He puts Himself in a place of need with her. He talks to her about the tensions and walls between Jews and Samaritans before He reveals His identity.

Jesus's patient tenderness toward the Samaritan woman reorients me. I read the passage again and again. Did you know the Samaritans and Jews were enemies who had been violently at odds for centuries? They could not agree to disagree. Their history was full of violence, hatred, deep distrust, and destruction. When the disciples arrive, flabbergasted to find Jesus talking to this person, not only does He stretch their perspectives about what's possible but He stretches their tenderness with His own. And then they all stay in Sychar for two more days—sleeping near, eating with, and choosing to know and be known by people they would have been taught to see as enemies.

Jesus never asks any of us to muster up our own tenderness; He knows we'd never have enough. He only tells us to follow and abide in the abundance of His tenderness.

Sandy and I have had to navigate how to remain for each other, for our friendship, and for our families, despite so many hard decisions for her family and mine—decisions that haven't always seemed compatible within our friendship. At some points it probably would've been easier to make a clean break, distancing ourselves from each other, numbing the painful feelings that come from loss and change. Instead, we've worked to keep tending each other's wounds and turning toward the difficulties we both face. In this case, our tenderness toward each other has looked less like superficial words of positivity and more like letting go, being honest, and staying patient. It looks like asking God for His tenderness when the pain pokes at our hearts and tempts us to let them become stiff, choosing instead to turn toward each other despite the raw edges of our different choices and needs.

My guess is that you also have relationships with raw edges. It's hard to be tender when those edges rub against each other. But maybe that's the gift of this long and unwanted season—being forced to learn new ways to sit with old friends.

Sandy and I don't show up to the same building for church anymore, but what I've come to realize and witness is this: when we walk together in one of our neighborhoods or meet for coffee, when we persist in tenderness toward each other, pray for people we know, or gather our families, we are being the church. It's been healing for me to take a step back and realize it was never about this church or that one but about each of us being the church Jesus intends us to be. I keep looking back at the fogginess of the last few years, asking God to show me where He was. I replay the events month by month. I feel the sadness, but I also see an audacious hope and a faithful perseverance in so many small things that can only come from Him.

Our daughter received a colorful stack of origami paper for her birthday in the spring of 2021. The first time she tried to fold one, she gave up. She crumpled the yellow paper, saying it wouldn't work, that the instructions tricked her, and she threw her attempt to the ground. I recognized my own temptation toward weariness in her expression—only my weariness and desire to give up had to do with relationships, loss, and responding to hurt. I couldn't help but think of the cranes we had made the year before. I listened to my own voice as I instinctively told her, "The special thing about this kind of paper is what also makes it difficult: it's fragile, and the creases stick, don't they? It's been made to fold easily, which means it breaks easily, and that's what makes origami so beautiful."

The fragility of this paper art makes it dependent on the tenderness of the hands that hold it. I told her to be gentle and patient with herself because that would help her to be gentle and patient with the paper. I told her that each time she shows up to try again, she's giving this paper bird (and with it, all of us) a chance to fly.

Questions to Sit With

Ask Yourself

1. How does my heart need to be more tender in friendships and relationships that have changed or navigated hardship?
2. How does Jesus model tenderness toward others in shocking ways?

3. Read John 4. What fruit and beauty come from Jesus's tenderness toward the Samaritan woman at the well and His tenderness toward you?

Ask God

1. God, show me Your tender heart toward me.
2. God, show me the hard, bitter places in my heart.
3. God, how do You want me to move forward with tenderness?

13

The Messy, Beautiful Power of Speaking the Truth in Love

Holley Gerth

My daughter sits across the table with her arms crossed, lips pursed, a frown crinkling her lovely forehead. I know that look—she's a volcano holding back from exploding. Until today, I've just never been the potential target.

Let me back up a bit to tell you how we got here. You might imagine this is a scene of teenage rebellion, the normal mother-daughter angst. But my daughter didn't even come into our lives until she was twenty years old. Yes, you read that right: *twenty*.

When Mark and I married, we thought having a family would come as easily for us as it seemed to for everyone else. But months of me peeing on sticks and ugly crying in bathrooms turned into years. I mourned, raged, and asked God hard questions. Then one night I watched a documentary about foster kids who age out of the system. At eighteen they're basically told, "Goodbye. Have a nice life." Everything in me said that's *not* okay.

So when people asked me if we ever thought about adoption, I'd answer, "If we adopt, our kid will be a twenty-year-old." One day a friend responded, "Have you heard about Saving Grace?" It turned out that a transitional home for girls who have aged out of the foster system or would otherwise be homeless was soon opening in our town.

I connected with the founder of Saving Grace, and years later she invited me to attend a banquet celebrating the accomplishments of the girls. That evening I met Lovelle, a fiery, resilient, bighearted twenty-year-old. Over the next few months, God made it clear that we were to be a family.

Now, years later, we sat across from each other in our first big fight. I cried, pounded the table with my fists, and even said a few choice words. I wanted to run. I felt like throwing up. I kept telling myself, "You've worked so hard for all these years to earn her trust and now you've blown it."

I grew up as a sweet Christian girl who was taught (whether directly or implied) that conflict is not okay, anger is a sin, and the best way to love people is to keep your mouth shut. Lovelle had already been through so much; I just wanted to protect her. But no relationship is perfect, and ours came with extra layers of complexity. So I quietly stored away unshared feelings, unaddressed issues, and unvoiced concerns, until one day they all came spilling out.

Somehow we wrestled our way through all of it. At the end I watched my daughter's shoulders drop, and I waited for words like, "You've really hurt me." Instead, she said with a relieved grin, "I feel really loved!"

Um, you what? I had no place for this conclusion in my universe, no explanation, no way to categorize or make sense of what she just said. I thought allowing myself to express emotions, hurts, and frustrations would damage our relationship. Instead, from her viewpoint, it showed my passion and commitment to our bond. If I, who avoided conflict, would go through that for her, then it must mean I really cared.

I didn't break her trust in me. By showing her we could disagree and still love each other, I built it.

I didn't fail to protect her by telling the truth. The only harm I did was in waiting so long to have the conversation.

I didn't wound our relationship. I strengthened it by showing her that no matter what happened, we would work through it together.

Come Sit with Me and Learn Together

Most of us have heard the phrase "speak the truth in love" (Eph. 4:15). Sadly, these days it's often used when someone is speaking the truth but *not* with love—the social media rant, critical remark, or judgmental evaluation of someone who's different from us. However, the opposite—speaking with love *but not the truth*—is just as harmful, and I was guilty of it. To see if you might be doing the same, read the following statements and notice if they ring true for you too:

- When I'm frustrated, I try to just get over it instead of working through it with the other person.
- When I'm hurt, I hold it inside rather than risk being vulnerable with the other person.

- I build up resentment because I think the other person should know what they've done without me needing to tell them.
- I sacrifice my own needs in the relationship because I'm afraid expressing them will inconvenience or distress the other person.
- I have the unrealistic expectation that a strong, long-term relationship can exist without conflict.

Since the day Lovelle and I had our fight, we've talked a lot about different communication styles. She grew up in an environment where communication was much more direct (although sometimes destructive). She asked an interesting question about my indirect style of communication: "Isn't that kind of like lying?" I'd never thought about it that way, but yes, she was on to something.

Just a few verses after Paul tells the Ephesians to "speak the truth in love," he also says, "So stop telling lies. Let us tell our neighbors the truth, for we are all parts of the same body" (Eph. 4:25 NLT). Sometimes a lie sounds like telling your boss you never got that important email—when you really did. But other times it sounds like "I'm fine" (when we're not) or "That's totally okay" (when it isn't) or "Sure, I understand" (when we don't).

One reason many of us struggle with more direct communication is because we've been told it's not okay to be angry. But in the very next verse Paul says, "Don't sin by letting anger control you" (v. 26 NLT). Anger is actually a useful emotion. It tells us when something we value is being threatened. It's a great messenger but a terrible boss. We're not to deny our anger; we're to direct it in constructive ways.

Paul gives further instructions by adding, "Don't let the sun go down while you are still angry" (v. 26 NLT). I don't believe this is a literal time limit. Sometimes a good night's sleep is essential to effectively addressing conflict. Instead, it's a principle—don't let what makes you angry go unresolved. That includes the seemingly tamer versions of anger like frustration and resentment. Why? "Anger gives a foothold to the devil" (v. 27 NLT). Unresolved anger in our relationships gives darkness a place that rightfully belongs to the light.

From a practical perspective, here are three steps that can help us speak the truth in love rather than stay silent in fear and resentment.

First, *identify expectations.* Anger in relationships often comes from unmet expectations we don't even know we have. We need to recognize those and then either release the other person from them or directly express those expectations as a request.

Second, *address issues as they come up.* Often what's happening is simply a misunderstanding. Everyone usually has good intentions, just not always great communication. When we talk about it, we can get clarity and move forward instead of getting stuck.

Third, *relentlessly be for each other.* Even when we're mad at someone, we can remember we're on the same side. The issue is what we're up against, not each other. Avoid harmful attacks like accusations, condemnation, or name-calling.

Lovelle will still occasionally say, "Remember when we had that fight? It was my favorite." And I will shake my head all over again because I'm still trying to make sense of how that can be true. Yet, when I look back, I can clearly see that conversation as a breakthrough. Since then, we've both worked hard to communicate better so we don't need to repeat that scenario. But it taught me an important lesson: trying to protect someone by holding back what really needs to be said is actually more likely to cause them pain.

I'm learning that sometimes the most dangerous choice we can make in our relationships is to settle for being "nice." Niceness often comes from fear; kindness comes from love. As followers of Jesus, we are being called to the latter.

May God grant us the courage to have hard conversations.

May He give us the inner strength to be vulnerable with each other.

May He help us trade resentments for life-giving, honest relationships.

May He even use our anger as a sacred, healing force in this world.

May He empower us to sit together and speak the truth in love.

Questions to Sit With

Ask Yourself

1. What's something I was taught about communication and relationships that might not be helpful? (Example: It's not okay to have conflict.)

2. When did having an honest, open conversation make a relationship in my life stronger, even if it was difficult to do?

3. What's one way I can speak the truth in love this week?

Ask God

1. God, where am I holding back out of fear rather than moving toward others with truth and love?
2. How do You want me to use my words to bring healing this week?
3. God, I want to be honest with You too. Thank You that I can share anything with You. Here's something hard I've been dealing with or feeling . . .

14

The Loving Work of Biting Your Tongue

Mary Carver

We were hiding from the heat, sisters in solidarity against vacationing in places that felt as hot as the surface of the sun. While most of our friends lounged by the pool, living their best lives with umbrella drinks and beach reads, the four of us sought refuge in the blessedly air-conditioned hotel room. In the privacy of that room, we could finally admit that we were melting and a little bit hangry (hot + angry) about it.

As we commiserated and cooled off, our conversation quickly turned to deeper topics.

I can still see us in that room, two of us on each of the two beds, facing each other and slowly getting comfortable. I'm not sure how we got from "I cannot deal with this heat" to "Some spaces aren't safe for people who look like me," but we did. Of the four of us friends, one was Black and one was Asian American. As they began to share their lived experiences in the world and on the internet, I was stunned.

Listening to their stories, I was shocked both by what I was hearing and learning and by my own reaction. At one point I sat on my hands in an attempt to remind myself to stay quiet and listen. I'd never before taken the phrase "bite your tongue" as literal advice, but as I felt objections rattling in my throat, I wondered if I would need to actually do it.

Internally I screamed, "But I'm not like that!" I longed to say, "I would never treat you like that—and I'm so mad that someone did!" Words of encouragement and empathy tend to be my friendship superpower, but somehow I knew this wasn't the time. Somehow I sensed that my expressing rage on my friends' behalf wasn't what was needed. It wouldn't help, and it might even hurt.

I sat in that hotel room in the summer of 2017, listening to my friends talk and carefully asking follow-up questions. It took restraint that I don't normally exercise, discernment and discipline that can only be attributed to the Holy Spirit. And not only did God make it clear that I should talk less and listen more but He also helped me hear something new, something heart-changing.

When I heard my friends say that they didn't feel welcome in communities that included very few people of color, my gut reaction was to yell, "But you *are* welcome! I promise! I want you there! You *should* feel welcome there!" I don't think that reaction was completely wrong, but it was coming from a place of ignorance. I didn't know what I didn't know, but from that conversation and many more since then, I began to learn.

Come Sit with Me and Learn Together

I've learned that I really don't understand what it's like to be a person of color in the United States. I've learned that having and loving friends from different cultural backgrounds doesn't mean I know what it's like to walk in their shoes. And as much as I've wanted to say, "We're all the same!" and move on, glossing over our differences downplays the pain and struggle and the beauty of those very differences. I've learned that just because I'm not overtly racist doesn't mean I don't have biases or that I don't benefit from a system rooted in racist assumptions and misunderstandings about people who are different from me.

I've learned that I have a lot to learn, and I won't be able to do that if I open my mouth and shout, "Not me!" and "Not every . . . !" each time the issue of race comes up. I've learned that feeling things in my heart is a good start, but it doesn't actually help my sisters and brothers of color. Well-intentioned emotions aren't enough.

We have to actually sit down together and listen. Sit on your hands if you need to. Bite your tongue if that's what it takes to stop yourself from interjecting or refuting what you're hearing, and just listen. I'm not saying this is easy, my friend. As a white woman, it's not easy for me to open up my mind and heart to recognize the injustices in this world, things that I simply wasn't aware of or unintentionally turned a blind eye to. It's not easy to sit in the tension of what the world is like and how I wish it would be. And I can only imagine that for my sisters and brothers of color it's not easy to vulnerably share their stories of encountering racism. It can't be easy to trust that you'll be believed and not questioned, fully accepted and not secretly rejected.

Sitting together on hotel beds or around dining tables, in conference rooms or church pews and really listening to others whose experiences are unlike our own isn't easy. But easy isn't the point. The point is connection. The point is loving one another well.

We have the privilege and responsibility of acknowledging the past and present wounds of the marginalized in our communities so we can begin to understand the depth and breadth of someone else's lived experience.

But understanding is just the first step—albeit a steeper one than I'd previously imagined. Because of my friends' honesty and the prompting of the Holy Spirit, I've come to understand that I can *and should* take action in creating a world that's welcoming and safe for all.

That day opened my eyes to the struggles and pain my friends (and others) face. It enabled me to evaluate issues I had not understood and problems I had not considered up to that point. Our conversation changed me and continues to change me. It was the beginning of my realization that simply feeling sad about racism and shouting supportive words aren't enough to make a difference. It's a privilege to listen and hold my friends' stories, and I'm grateful that in His love, God revealed the ways my posture, my beliefs, and my actions needed to change so I can truly love others as He does.

Fast-forward to today, and God has been faithfully persistent in teaching me that embracing and celebrating the diversity of His people *is* how I can see Him more fully. Through reading books, watching movies, and listening to the stories shared by my fellow (in)courage sisters, I'm being humbled and keeping my heart soft. I'm learning to sit in the discomfort of being challenged on my long-held perspectives and knee-jerk reactions, I'm having hard but good conversations with my kids, and I'm doing the long-term work of justice in my everyday life.

I don't always get it right, but that's part of the growth process. We learn. We mess up. We do our best to make things right. And we keep going.

Questions to Sit With

Ask Yourself

1. How can I make space for others to share their experiences?
2. What are my tendencies when others are sharing something that makes me feel uncomfortable or that I don't agree with?
3. How can I do a better job of listening to others when they share stories of pain or injustice?

Ask God

1. God, reveal to me any biases or beliefs that keep me from loving others well.
2. What's one small step You want me to take today to engage in the work of justice?
3. What does it look like to fully embrace, celebrate, and advocate for the complete body of Christ?

15

Exchanging Envy for Celebration

Aliza Latta

I brought a rush of hot, summer air with me as I walked through my friend's front door. I turned the corner down her hall, and there they were: my friend, just a handful of days postpartum, and her tiny child sleeping wrapped against her chest. Tears blurred my vision. I often cry when my friends have babies.

When she first told me she was pregnant, I had burst into tears. We were in my car on our way to a friend's house when she pulled out her sonogram and held it up to show me. She said, "There's someone I'd like you to meet." I almost swerved into oncoming traffic, then yanked the steering wheel toward a nearby parking lot and thrust the car into park. Tears dripped down my cheeks as I held the black-and-white photo in my hands. It was hard for me to fathom—there was a tiny person growing within my friend at that very moment.

"Sorry for telling you while you were driving." She smiled sheepishly.

I just laughed, brushing the tears away. "*You,*" I told her with utter sincerity, "are going to be a wonderful mother."

It was true—motherhood was embedded in her DNA. But I wasn't sure if it was embedded in mine. I didn't know if I was nurturing or organized enough to keep a child alive. But she was; I was confident of that.

As I rounded the corner on that late summer morning to meet her days-old son, something lurched within my chest. The baby we had long awaited was finally here. A month earlier we had celebrated with a baby shower and gifts and cards. Just a week earlier, in my small apartment, we had prayed protection and safety over her labor and delivery. My hands had gently rested on her swollen belly as I asked the Holy Spirit to be present as her child entered our world.

Now, my friend stood up from her chair, a smile stretching across her cheeks, and placed the baby in my arms. I sat on her leather couch and stared at him, overwhelmed by his presence despite how little space he took up in my arms. He was light, precious. I couldn't get over how tiny his nose was, or how I could feel his lips blowing the smallest stream of air each time he exhaled.

"Wow," I said. "He's all yours."

For the next hour she recounted her birth story. She wasn't tired like I expected. She was vibrant and energized, as if motherhood had given her distinct purpose and a reason for being on this earth. Her face was awash with color; she bounced around the room even though she had given birth just a few days earlier. She was a woman who had partaken in the miracle of childbirth, and the adrenaline was still coursing through her body.

I held her son in silence while she spoke, my heart racing as I listened. I grew increasingly overwhelmed as she talked—like the very air was closing in on me. I returned the baby to her, and my arms felt empty and listless when I went to sit back on the couch by myself. I wished I still had him, if only to have something to hold.

The idea of childbirth wasn't new to me, but I couldn't wrap my head around what she was saying—about laboring, or the pain, or gripping her husband's hand so tightly he almost passed out. With each word she spoke, the lurching in my chest grew tighter and more pronounced. I didn't know what to say. Even though neither of us had acknowledged it, I knew everything had suddenly changed. I didn't know what she needed now that she had a baby. I didn't know what our friendship would look like now that she was a mother. A chasm had formed between us that I didn't know how to cross. My envy was thick, and the depth of my loneliness felt inescapable. My friend didn't know it then, but I wanted everything she seemed to have: a husband, a house, and now, a baby.

I wanted to celebrate with her, but I also wanted to leave. I sat on my hands instead. Eventually, I collected my purse and told her I should go. Her eyes were still radiant. She was in her own beautiful world, and she couldn't help but glow.

I hugged her, kissed the top of her child's head, and assured her to call me if she needed anything. Then I climbed into my car and cried.

I cried for all that I didn't have—and for fear of never having it.

"Jesus," I prayed as tears streamed down my cheeks, "I am so lonely. I'm so happy for her, but I'm so sad for myself. I want a husband. I want a baby. I want my friendships to stop changing. I want to trust You, but all I feel right now is pain."

My envy, pain, and loneliness crowded out my capacity for celebration. I didn't know how to hold my envy and her happiness together in my hands. I was watching the hopes and dreams I had for myself play out in someone else's life, and I was terrified that was the way it would always be.

I put my car in drive and cried the entire way home.

Come Sit with Me and Learn Together

I would've liked my envy and loneliness to be fixed with a marriage and children. I would've preferred God to hand me a husband the way someone hands me french fries at the drive-through window. I wanted to believe that marriage would satisfy my inner longings, that having a child would relieve the depth of my loneliness. But marriage and a baby haven't happened for me yet. (And yes, I know that neither of these things will truly cure my pain or loneliness.) Yet, for so long I kept my eyes fixed on my friends' lives. I felt like God was making all of their dreams come true and had somehow forgotten about me. Instead of keeping my eyes on Jesus and on the adventures He might have in store for me, I focused on what I didn't have.

The apostle Peter had a similar experience. He's one of my favorite disciples, mostly because he seems feisty and tender and makes thousands of mistakes, and yet Jesus knows that and chooses him anyway. Peter reminds me of me. In John

21, Peter and Jesus share a deeply personal moment that offers much healing and redemption. (You should just go ahead and read that chapter while we're talking about it. It's beautiful—all about a beach and breakfast and restoration.) But near the end of the chapter, Jesus gives Peter a glimpse of how he's going to die. Talk about intense. Peter doesn't know how to handle what Jesus tells him, so he awkwardly looks over at John and asks, "Lord, what about him?" (v. 21).

I imagine Jesus keeping His eyes on Peter as He replies, "If I want him to remain alive until I return, what is that to you? You must follow me" (v. 22).

I do this a lot. I look out at the world, and I see my friends getting married and having babies, and I feel my heart shatter a little with fear and loneliness, and I ask Jesus, "What about her? Why is her life going the way she wants it to? Why are her dreams coming true?"

And I think Jesus keeps His tender eyes trained on me and says with kindness, "What is that to you? You must follow Me."

You must follow Me.

Those words pierce me because they highlight my very real tendency to forget that, first and foremost, Jesus is the one I want to follow in my life. Instead, I find myself putting comparison or envy or pain in that first-place position. But Jesus hasn't called me to follow my friends. He hasn't even called me to necessarily follow my dreams. He's called me to follow *Him.*

The truth is, it's not about her. *Her* life is not my life (even if some days I wish it were). God has a creative, unique blueprint for each of us—which is good, because the world would be awfully boring if our lives were all the same. The life Jesus has for me is different from the life He has for you. He's given each of us different personalities, interests, quirks, cultural backgrounds, families of origin—all of which come with their own layers to wade through.

But through it all Jesus says, "Follow Me."

When we trust Jesus, we become free.

Free to live the lives and dream the dreams *He* has for us.

Free to celebrate what He has in store for our friends.

Free to rejoice instead of envy.

Even if it still hurts a little (which, in all honesty, it does), I can keep my eyes on Jesus through the pain. I can celebrate and rejoice with my friends over what God is doing in their lives—because I can choose to trust Him instead of envying others. Trust is more powerful and brave than envy anyway.

Envy is self-centered. Trust is generous.

Envy is fearful. Trust is courageous.

Envy sees only the negative. Trust chooses, over and over, to see the good.

My friend and I are both still in different seasons of life. But I am beginning to understand that our differences don't have to cause a chasm in our friendship. Instead, I can cross our new life-stage divide with arms wide open, ready to celebrate all God has for her and trusting Jesus has adventures in store for me. It turns out, my friend has a lot to offer me in her current season of marriage and motherhood. But the truth is, I have a lot to offer her too.

And if, in the midst of my celebration and trust, the envy and pain and loneliness still sneak in, I'll bring every ache into the light of Jesus. Because no matter what happens in the lives of the people around me, I'm choosing to follow Him.

Questions to Sit With

Ask Yourself

1. Where has envy, pain, or loneliness cropped up in my relationships?
2. What is holding me back from celebrating and rejoicing with friends for what God is doing in their lives?
3. What does it look like in my life to continue to choose to trust and follow Jesus?

Ask God

1. God, how can I practice keeping my eyes fixed on You instead of on the lives of others?
2. How do You want me to celebrate and rejoice with my friends?
3. Jesus, remind me that I can always bring every ache and every feeling of loneliness to You—no matter what.

16

Will You Be a Flamethrower or a Fire Extinguisher in the Dumpster Fire of Internet Comments?

Jami Nato

Several weeks ago, I opened my Instagram feed and noticed some weird activity on a video I had posted many months earlier. Forty-six thousand likes! *Have I been hacked?* As I clicked on the post, I realized that a fifteen-second video I had made of our neighborhood's summer block party had unexpectedly gone viral. *Wow! This is cool.*

The video wasn't anything special. Just a quick pan of the street from my front porch. Neighbors gathered around folding tables we had set up in the street and kids roamed in packs like happy wild animals. It was my attempt to share a glimpse of our neighborhood magic, and I wrote a quick caption with tips and encouragement to help others engage their neighbors too.

In it, I confessed my initial annoyance over moving to the suburbs. We were sophisticated "city people" who secretly thought we were more awesome than the suburbanites. Throw in a special needs kiddo and the need to move to a school system that was more accommodating, and you have a lady who needs to gently eat her words and say I was wrong.

I wrote how the suburb has been the sweetest teacher of community. I thought I knew what community was before, but I didn't. We moved in and were immediately welcomed into the dinner club that had been going on for twenty years, where everyone takes a turn (alphabetically) hosting a quarterly neighborhood dinner. Some bring out their best china, while others use paper plates. They have a seating arrangement and separate spouses so you have to get to know others (WHOA NOW!). It is actually so fun.

The kids will play so hard in the front yards, they forget to eat. We sometimes have freezer Fridays when everyone unloads forgotten frozen delights and the kids graze and make dance routines. They fight too; there's street justice out here. The ladies have a vibrant text strand for sharing memes or Maydays: "WHO HAS A TOMATO?!" Followed by, "Just dropped one off at your door." And of course there's the coping mechanism basket we pass around and fill up when someone is having a hard time.

I understand that it takes years to build this kind of life-together community; it starts with someone going first and taking a risk to even start a text strand. Or have your neighbors over for dinner. Or play in the front yard instead of the back. But good things take time. I encouraged my Instagram friends to stick with it. This neighborhood community is one of our greatest joys.[1]

With over two million views, this was obviously striking a chord with people. Again, my first reaction was "How cool!" Except it wasn't all cool.

Most of the comments rolling in were from complete strangers. Some of them were encouraging, but as the video went more viral, the comments became anonymous and cutting. For the next several days I had to be really vigilant to delete spammy comments like "DM me and I'll send you $3,000 tomorrow!" and biting comments like "Must be nice to live in an all-white neighborhood." My gut reaction was to spew back defensively that my husband is the first Filipino homeowners association president the neighborhood has had and that my Asian kids are the ones on the scooters there to the left. I want to point out Ms. Christina, who goes to the Asian market and brings us special candies and tiger balm every week.

But as I scrolled through nasty comments and messages about our neighborhood, our race, our demographic, all the unimportant and untrue things being assumed as fact on a post that was meant to stir up kindness, I realized I had to decide how I wanted to treat this dumpster fire.

I could defend myself and add fuel to the blaze. Or I could take a beat and let my pause extinguish the flames.

It would have been easy to get sucked into defending myself, to expend copious amounts of time communicating with strangers who troll the internet, people who don't know me

1. Jami Nato (@jaminato), Instagram, September 27, 2021, https://www.instagram.com/reel/CUVKgF5AM_p/.

or my family. I stopped myself at some point and thought, *Wait . . . I'm taking time and emotional energy away from the people I made the video about in the first place—my family, my neighbors, those right in front of me.*

It seems like more and more, anytime we open our phones and computers, we see someone's extreme opinions about the latest hot topic—which appears to be almost everything. What a time to be alive, when you can communicate your inner thoughts to pretty much anyone with the click of a Send button!

Chances are you've also experienced this phenomenon of the unfiltered response. Here's a simple example of how it might shake out:

Someone posts a photo of a bakery item the size of the moon next to a steaming cup of coffee, a pretty flower arrangement, and an open Bible. The caption reads: Look at this cinnamon roll!

Comment 1: Yum!

Comment 2: LOL, gluten is bad for you!

Comment 3: I ate a donut last week, and it gave me an infection in my big toe. Look at this! (photo attached)

Comment 4: My aunt was a donut maker, and she's also a [insert political affiliation], so we don't eat them anymore. No thanks, can't be associated with them!

Comment 5: Ok, HUMBLE brag with the Bible. 😳

I feel my chest tighten and notice I'm holding my breath. *Really? Was that necessary? I don't want to do this anymore.*

Come Sit with Me and Learn Together

Maybe we've always been this divided and just didn't know it. Now, with technology constantly at our fingertips, the divisiveness is glaring. I miss not knowing *how much* we are divided. I miss not being anxious about relational stress as we approach yet another election year, yet another global health issue, yet another this side versus that side. And before I can even formulate language to describe this anxiety, my body responds for me: I wear my shoulders as earmuffs. My breath quickens. I wince. My brow furrows, blood rushes to my cheeks, my stomach hurts. If you watch the news or have social media or talk to a neighbor, you probably know what I mean.

I close the computer and think about it all day. And "it" isn't just my video gone viral or the hypothetical cinnamon roll scenario. It's all the backhanded comments and jumping to false assumptions. It's the tearing down and creating us-versus-them categories for every possible issue. It's using our words as weapons and calling it normal. It's *all of it*. And I can't help but think, *I wish she hadn't mentioned that. I wish he hadn't said it in that way. They make me so mad. Why are people like this? Why can't we just stop treating each other like this?*

But the more I think about it, the more I think about the human condition we need saving from: our own selves. Before you throw tomatoes at me, I didn't come up with this idea. In the New Testament, James writes, "What causes quarrels and what causes fights among you? Is it not this, that your passions are at war within you? You desire and do not have, so you murder. You covet and cannot obtain, so you fight and quarrel" (James 4:1–2 ESV).

Ouch. That one convicted me so badly that I recently chose to memorize it to prepare myself each day before I open my computer. And let me say, when I'm about to actively run into an argument after reading Cousin Fred's entire comments section in his latest fire-breathing post, I instead take a deep breath and consume truth that comes from a living and active God. A God who loves me but isn't afraid to ask me to check my perspective.

So I pray, *I am the problem. Forgive me, Lord, for wanting to murder this person with my words, for believing I am more worthy of Your gift of grace than he is. Give me the supernatural power to love someone I think of as my enemy. I can't do this on my own.*

As believers, we should be people marked not by fear, hatred, or murderous words but by peace. We should desire unity instead of actively seeking out division with our words. We should have the markings of self-control and love, not unbridled tongues that have the power to set the world on fire (see James 3:5–6). I don't know if I really believed that until the last couple years, but haven't we all witnessed the destruction caused by our tongues and how they hold the power of life and death?

We each have personal accounts of our own fractured relationships and devastating losses. But lest this all start to feel a bit depressing, we actually do have great hope. Jesus tells us, "I have said these things to you, that in me you may have peace. In the world you will have tribulation. But take heart; I have overcome the world" (John 16:33 ESV).

Read that verse again. Hear Jesus speaking it to you: *"In Me you may have peace. Take heart."* Notice how your body responds to the truth. It's quite different from scrolling through a social media feed. Maybe, if you're like me, your shoulders come down and your breath slows. As the words of Scripture settle into my heart, I can see things more clearly: We are too quick to scroll conversations and comment threads and assume we are the only ones who know the correct path. But God is our Good Shepherd. He actively searches to bring us back to Himself, reorient our hearts toward Him, and give us the peace of His guidance, care, and protection—even from ourselves.

We are not on our own when we face difficult circumstances and interactions or when we have to navigate complex relationships and complicated feelings. When we see ourselves and others with the right perspective, we remember that our words, whether written in a comment or spoken out loud, have the power to attest to a better word: God is our only hope in this world. And what good news that it doesn't rest on our human shoulders!

Questions to Sit With

Ask Yourself

1. What is my posture when I read posts or comments online that I don't agree with?
2. Where am I tempted to use my words to tear down or divide instead of to build up and bring peace?

3. Who in my life, whether online or in everyday relationships, is hard to love? How can I use my words this week to esteem them?

Ask God

1. Lord, help me see the passions warring within me and replace them with Your peace.
2. God, what does it look like to take heart in You today?
3. How do You want me to use my words to point people to Your hope?

17

How to Carry the Weight of Rejection

Simi John

I couldn't stop crying. I didn't think it would hurt this much. I thought I would be used to it by now, but this time the cut felt deep. She was my friend. We had prayed together during difficult seasons and we had celebrated together at our kids' birthday parties. But when she decided to leave our church, she didn't mention it to me. She took the time to unfollow me on Instagram, unfriend me on Facebook, and unsubscribe from everything that connected me to her in any way. The reason she chose to leave had nothing to do with me, and she didn't want to talk to me about it. But the message she sent was loud and clear: *I don't want you or your church in my life.*

The weight of rejection slowly began to break me. But I was the pastor's wife, so I had to be strong and smile. I didn't have a place where I could really share my emotions and process the situation. I wanted to look unfazed because this type of rejection is just part of being in ministry. People come and go all the time, but this time it felt different because the person was actually my friend. She didn't just leave our church. She left me.

Relationships are complex and humans are complicated, so rejection is part of life. It doesn't just happen on the playground in elementary school or when your crush doesn't ask you to prom or when the college you want to attend puts you on their wait list. Rejection follows us into adulthood as we navigate relationships and community. Sometimes people will just walk out with no warning and no resolution. I don't know about you, but it bothers me to have things left unresolved—kind of like when people forget to close the cabinet doors. It creates a sense of internal stress and chaos. We prefer if our conflicts can be wrapped up with a pretty bow, but sometimes there is no closure. I know this, yet when my friend didn't want to have a conversation to close the chapter on our friendship, I felt a surge of anxiety.

My mind rushed to think of all the possible reasons she couldn't talk to me, couldn't say a proper goodbye—but I came up empty. I went through a season of anger because I felt it was unfair for her to treat me this way. I went through weeks of grief as her rejection finally left me numb.

Come Sit with Me and Learn Together

Rejection is hard for the heart to handle. We come into the world wanting to be held, loved, and seen. These hardwired needs are part of survival. As human beings, we all have an innate need to belong. So when we feel rejected, we usually also feel alone in the world and therefore try to protect ourselves. This can lead us to mistrust others, avoid being vulnerable, and strive to win people's approval. In the aftermath of my friend's rejection, I was going down this path of self-preservation.

In my pain I made a decision to put up my guard in every future relationship. I told myself that as a pastor's wife, I should hold everyone at arm's length and never again let anyone close enough that they could hurt me so deeply. Immediately after I made this decision, the Holy Spirit impressed these words on my heart: "That is not the way I love you!"

I argued back, "If I want to survive in ministry for the long haul, I have to protect myself from people hurting and leaving me."

And then in the gentlest way He reminded me, "Simi, you hurt Me, you ignore Me, and you have rejected My voice, but I still love you the same. If you want to lead My people, you have to love them like I do—that is what it means to be a shepherd."

I felt something shift inside me in that moment, and I surrendered the pain and hurt to Jesus. I released my friend and my unforgiveness to God. That day I decided to always keep my heart soft and my people close. It may be hard and I may get hurt again, but I always want to be vulnerable enough to deeply embrace and love God's people. I know that when I do, He will defend and protect my heart.

I made up my mind that I will not try to avoid rejection, because honestly, that would be impossible unless I were to live as a hermit. But I will rest in the finished work of Christ who calls me accepted and approved. When rejection comes, I stand firm in the unchanging truth of God's Word. Then I am able to continue living authentically and vulnerably without needing to protect myself or prove my worth to others.

This experience also helped me to understand that relationships have seasons. People will naturally come and go. Our preferences change as we grow, so we must learn that a person's behavior or choice isn't necessarily a reflection on us. What if we chose not to take it personally when we experience rejection or when the seasons of friendship shift? Sometimes we might bear the brunt of a person's unhappiness or anger, but that doesn't mean we're actually the cause of it. We have to choose to look beyond the problem and allow the other person space to process instead of rushing to fix the issue.

Relationships will always be risky. But isn't that true of everything in life that is worth our time and investment? God has called us to relationship with Him and with others. So even as I take the risk of walking in community with others, God is walking with me. I lean on Him for wisdom and discernment on how to set boundaries, when to be vulnerable, and how to forgive.

Maybe for you it's a family member who left, a friend who ghosted you, or a boss who overlooked you. Whatever the source of the rejection, the pain is real. Sometimes there is no real solution to the issue, but you still have a choice in how you respond.

In the book of Romans, Paul writes, "Live in harmony with each other. . . . Never pay back evil with more evil. Do things in such a way that everyone can see you are honorable. Do all that you can to live in peace with everyone" (12:16–18 NLT). Notice how Paul says we must *do all we can* to live at peace with everyone. This is an incredibly important distinction, because it helps us recognize that while we are responsible for our own actions, we are not responsible for how others respond. You can control whether or not you pay back evil for evil, gossip for gossip, insult for insult, slander for slander. You can control whether or not you behave in a way that is honorable, even when someone hurts you intentionally or treats you unfairly. However, you cannot control how another person thinks or behaves.

You may do everything you possibly can to try and live in peace with another person, but they still may not desire to have a relationship with you. They may mistreat you or walk out of your life. In these instances you might not have closure, but you can have internal peace. Peace comes when you're living out God's will for your life. Regardless of how others respond, God will honor your commitment to live in harmony and to love them well.

Even Jesus, the perfect Son of God who lived a blameless life, was rejected. Jesus modeled how to respond to rejection and live at peace with others. Many times in the Gospels we see Jesus walking away in silence, and He teaches His disciples to "shake off the dust from your feet" when faced with rejection (Matt. 10:14 ESV). In order for us to live at peace with those who have rejected us, we have to learn to shake it off. Don't gossip about it with others; don't slander your offender's name. We don't always need to argue and debate to make others understand our perspective. Rather, in humility we can choose to walk away, shake it off, and move on. Because Jesus experienced rejection, He empathizes with us and can give us comfort and strength to move through it.

Friend, if you are hurting today, if you are feeling the sting of rejection or the pain of a broken relationship, be assured of this: God sees you, and He is working through you.

Receive these words from Paul as you let God carry the weight of rejection with you:

> May God our Father and the Lord Jesus Christ give you grace and peace. All praise to God, the Father of our Lord Jesus Christ. God is our merciful Father and the source of all comfort. He comforts us in all our troubles so that we can comfort others. When they are troubled, we will be able to give them the same comfort God has given us. (2 Cor. 1:2–4 NLT)

Questions to Sit With

Ask Yourself

1. Am I holding a grudge against someone who has hurt me in the past?
2. How might I need to make amends with someone for repaying hurt for hurt?
3. Is there a relationship that I've been trying to hold on to that I need to shake off and walk away from? If so, what first step can I take?

Ask God

1. Lord, show me the people toward whom I harbor unforgiveness or bitterness.
2. Lord, how I can exemplify Your love and patience to those who have hurt me?
3. Lord, teach me to rest in Your acceptance and love and not require the approval of others.

18

The Question That Changes Everything

Robin Dance

My father's third wedding was neither fancy nor typical. His bride-to-be, Alice, wore a nondescript tea-length dress, and instead of a candlelit sanctuary with a flower-adorned altar, she had chosen her mother's carport as the venue. Attendees stood under a ceiling laced in cobwebs and crinkled with age. No bridesmaids, no groomsmen, and no frills, but the bride carried a lovely bouquet. Thankfully, the weather cooperated for this outdoor occasion because there was no plan B.

Alice's walk down the aisle consisted of seven steps from the back door to where my father stood awaiting her. As it turned out, her bridal march was not only short but also comical and one of the most memorable moments of the entire ceremony. Alice had purchased a CD to play for the processional but had forgotten her old boom box only had a cassette deck. Quick thinking by my brother saved the day. He pulled his shiny sports car next to the makeshift altar, rolled down his windows, and cranked up the volume on his custom audio system. That car stereo was the fanciest part of the whole wedding.

At some point after the bride and groom said "I do," my grown siblings and I shuffled our dad into a corner and asked him if he and Alice had signed a prenuptial agreement. Our tact and timing may have been lousy, but our concern was valid. His marital track record didn't give us much hope for his third attempt. We were also protective of what he had accomplished over a lifetime of hard work and how a new spouse might affect his future.

Daddy didn't appreciate the intrusion into his personal life.

It wasn't that my sister, brothers, and I didn't want Daddy to be happy, but none of us were thrilled about his marriage. To begin with, Alice was only five years older than I was, and though she looked and acted like someone closer to my father's age, we were wary. We simply couldn't understand their attraction to each other. We had tried to get to know her while they were dating, but our relationships remained surface level and polite.

To be fair, circumstances made it difficult to forge any real relationship with Alice. My sister and I were both married and living out of town, and my younger brothers weren't interested. Our personalities were so different that, even if we had met under different circumstances, I wouldn't have been drawn to her in friendship. On the flip side, Alice didn't put forth much effort either. Given our ages and stage in life, there wasn't any expectation of bonding as a stepmother and child. She was always and only my father's wife.

I loved my father, and dearly so, but as many father-daughter relationships go, ours was complex. He carried heavy baggage from his own family's dysfunction while he was growing up, as well as enormous guilt over divorcing Mama in the midst of her battle with cancer. My dad was a man who had difficulty expressing his emotions, and yet somehow he managed to always make me feel smart and beautiful and loved. I respected how he cared for me and my siblings in the wake of our mother's death when I was just nine.

No doubt Daddy and I loved each other, but we didn't share one of those syrupy father-daughter relationships. I suspect the desire was there, but during my high school and college years I lacked the maturity and experience to bridge our gaps, and he simply wasn't equipped to cultivate a deeply emotional connection. I think he tried to in his own way. He ended every phone conversation we ever had with, "I love you. Call me anytime." His way of inviting more connection.

As months bled into years, Daddy and Alice surpassed my low expectations and remained committed to each other "for better or worse." Alice navigated Daddy's cantankerous and curmudgeonly disposition with acceptance, accommodation, and remarkably good cheer. However, their age difference became more pronounced when Daddy's health began to falter. His occasional spells of forgetfulness worsened into larger memory issues that became the norm.

If you've ever had someone you love fall prey to dementia, you know it's a wicked disease that plunders the mind and leaves behind a cruel vacancy. The person is physically present, but everything that makes them who they are slowly trickles away.

Motivated by the love she had for him, Alice downplayed Daddy's symptoms at first, enabling or accommodating his whims and wishes. Eventually, though, denial was no longer an option. After a catastrophic reaction to a drug that had been prescribed to calm him, Daddy's illness escalated to an extreme. He almost died that day, and had we understood what the future held for our father, we would have prayed for death's mercy rather than for God to spare him.

Overnight, Daddy went from being able to do just about everything for himself to needing assistance with every daily activity. The last fourteen months of his life were a nightmare— both for him and for his family, though each in different ways. His particular form of dementia brought with it hallucinations and fitful sleep, if he slept at all. He battled demons we couldn't see.

Daddy needed care (or at least a watchful eye) around the clock. Our family stepped in as often as we could, but we also needed the help of paid professionals. Alice coordinated the calendar to make sure someone was always by his side. I think I had romanticized what a parent-child role reversal might look like, but those notions were crushed as we cared for his most personal needs. The indignity of it was awful.

An old proverb says, "Adversity makes strange bedfellows," and this was certainly true for my family in that season. Everyone who loved Daddy—me, my three siblings, Alice, and even Daddy's second wife (my stepmom, who still had feelings for him)—all had different opinions about what was best for him. We didn't always agree, and having conversations about his care often felt like navigating a war zone. Tiptoeing around land mines is exhausting.

I remember one afternoon when I was venting to my husband, frustrated and angry that my father's choices in marriage were impacting my life in maddening and inconvenient ways. Never one to tell me what I want to hear, Tad's response was jarring but effective: "If God has brought these people into your life, don't you think He has a good reason?" He let the question linger, patiently awaiting my response, as nothing and everything changed.

Come Sit with Me and Learn Together

Sometimes I'm tempted to compartmentalize my faith, living it out when it's easy, when it's convenient, or when it falls within the boundaries of my comfort zone. In his letter to the Philippians, Paul instructs, "In humility value others above yourselves" (2:3). My disobedience is subtle but undeniable when I refuse to submit to what God asks of me. But there are no loopholes in His Word that allow me to pick and choose who I love and how I love them. God calls us to love all people at all times and to maintain peace so far as it depends on us (Rom. 12:18).

Daddy's illness had bound together a group of people with diverse personalities and varied opinions who all loved him and needed to work together. Barring a miracle, my dad's health was not going to improve. The circumstances we found ourselves in were not going to change. The situation seemed to be spinning out of control, and I had been ricocheting between feelings of helplessness, exasperation, and anger.

If God has brought these people into your life, don't you think He has a good reason?

Tad's question was a glass of cold water splashing my face, reminding me of who I am and Whose I am: a daughter of God, wholly loved, saved by His magnificent grace, and called to love Him and others. As I pondered God's purposes in that season, the Holy Spirit reminded me that while I couldn't control the circumstances, I *could* control my response to them.

So, I began looking at the people God was bringing into my life because of Daddy's illness—not just his wife and our family but also a parade of caregivers—as opportunities for me to reflect His glory, to share how the life, death, and resurrection of Jesus have impacted my life (the good news of the gospel!), and to love them because they also were hurting.

This doesn't mean that difficult-for-me-to-love people were suddenly my new best friends. But as I earnestly prayed that God would transform me into a new person by changing the way I think (see Rom. 12:2 NLT), He did. As I shifted the focus from me and my mixed bag of emotions to God and what His purposes might be, my heart was filled with compassion and a supernatural love for others.

Undoubtedly, there have been (or are or will be) difficult people and painful circumstances in your life. Perhaps you have a zealous family member or friend whose opinions differ so greatly from your own on politics or the pandemic or other hot-button issues that your relationship has been battered and bruised. Maybe a coworker who feels threatened by your strengths undermines you in front of others. Or maybe you have a child who is making destructive choices that adversely impact your entire family. When we inevitably find ourselves in these and other scenarios, the question to ask is, "How am I responding?"

Can I be that sister-friend who gently poses the question, "If God has brought these people into your life, don't you think He has a good reason?"

Reframing how you view hard and heartbreaking relationships or other life challenges changes everything.

Questions to Sit With

Ask Yourself

1. Which people in my life do I have a hard time loving?
2. How am I thinking more highly of myself than others, and how might I serve them better?
3. What are some practical changes I can make to strengthen my faith and grow closer to God? How might that impact my relationships with others?

Ask God

1. What sin in my own heart is hindering me from loving others?
2. What hard circumstances in my life are opportunities in disguise to reflect Your goodness and glory?
3. Who have You brought into my life that needs to hear the gospel?

19

Staying Curious When You Want to Run Away

Michele Cushatt

We'd been dating for several months when he dropped the bombshell.

In all fairness, he didn't realize it was a bombshell. He just shared his political leanings, including how he and his family of origin typically voted in local, state, and national elections. It was a random conversation, nothing emotionally charged. Nothing to indicate a significant shift. Just information shared in passing between two people who were dating but still getting to know each other.

The problem? I was raised in a family that was rooted firmly and squarely in the opposing party.

I don't remember how the conversation even started, but I do remember where we were and how I felt when it happened. The moment he identified his political affiliation, I felt like I had been slapped. We stood on opposite sides of an impossible war. There was no reconciling this difference. As much as we had in common, including our Christian faith, this was a massive and unbreachable divide. And just that fast, I considered ending our relationship. How could we possibly move forward?

I'm a bit embarrassed now to admit how shocked and appalled I felt at learning his political affiliation. I thought he was a good Christian man who loved Jesus and tried to follow Him in his day-to-day life. How could he side with a political party that seemed to be clearly on the opposing side? How could he identify with any party other than the one I voted for? My family history is thick with patriotism and men who served our country in the military during multiple international wars. I respected these relatives of mine, both living and deceased. A sense of national pride was core to my family's identity. With one simple, offhand admission, my view of this person—as a man, a potential husband, and a believer—completely changed.

With the benefit of hindsight, I'm surprised how quickly I devalued and disregarded him because of our apparent political differences. To my young and idealistic self, this was a deal breaker, a relationship ender. There was only one seemingly right answer to this test question, and he'd answered incorrectly. Because I equated real faith with a specific political party, his political leanings made me question the legitimacy of his faith and thus the legitimacy of our relationship. And somewhere along the way I'd come to believe you could only be in a deep and meaningful relationship with people you agreed with, especially about something this important.

When I told him as much, his face mirrored my own shock, but for a different reason. He couldn't understand my disappointment or the arrogance and judgment that came packaged in my voting record. At first he thought I must be joking. Then his chuckle of laughter turned defensive. I don't blame him. My rejection of him as a person had been quick and complete and was because of something he didn't believe warranted such a divide.

By some minor miracle of grace, he forgave my arrogance and we continued the conversation. And it's a good thing, too, because we've enjoyed a beautiful marriage together for more than two decades now. In those twenty years, we've walked through many elections and even more conversations. And I came to discover, not long after that initial conversation, that we had far more commonalities than differences when it came to our convictions. He was indeed a man of deep faith, a faith that in many ways was stronger than my own. I just hadn't withheld my judgment long enough to stay engaged, to connect, and to listen.

Over the years we've both changed our political affiliation, and our voting history has grown and matured as we have. In addition, we now share six children, three of whom are well into adulthood. And nearly every time the eight of us gather for a holiday or family meal, the conversation invariably turns to topics that reveal our obvious differences, political and otherwise. Every time it does, I'm grateful I'm not the same young idealist who was willing to abandon a relationship with someone I love simply because we disagreed.

It's good to be principled, to hold deep convictions and live them out with consistency and passion. But when we love our principles and positions to the exclusion of the people standing right in front of us, we've lost sight of the gospel— our good news. You see, Jesus entered into relationship with us when we were actively rebelling against Him. We stood on the opposite side of an impossible divide. There was no way to reach a compromise, no negotiating or converting. We were separated, completely and irrevocably. He had every right to exact judgment and walk away, to let us die in our isolation. He was 100 percent in the right, and we were 100 percent in the wrong.

But rather than walking away, Jesus walked toward, knowing we could do nothing to bridge the divide ourselves. Romans 5:8 says, "But God demonstrates his own love for us in this: While we were still sinners, Christ died for us." Jesus chose to reconcile us to God at His own cost, taking on Himself the judgment we deserved. Why? Because He loves us.

Instead of rejection, grace. Instead of punishment, love.

> Who shall separate us from the love of Christ? Shall trouble or hardship or persecution or famine or nakedness or danger or sword? . . . No, in all these things we are more than conquerors through him who loved us. For I am convinced that neither death nor life, neither angels nor demons, neither the present nor the future, nor any powers, neither height nor depth, nor anything else in all creation, will be able to separate us from the love of God that is in Christ Jesus our Lord. (Rom. 8:35, 37–39)

Because of a grace we don't deserve and a love we'll never be able to repay, we're forever joined with the Lover of our souls. A relationship that was once irreconcilable is now unbreakable. It's sure and steadfast, no matter how many times we fail. May our awareness of this love increase our capacity to offer it to others, in spite of our differences, with the same boundless and bridging grace.

Come Sit with Me and Learn Together

Staying engaged in conversation with someone you disagree with is difficult under any circumstances, but even more so when the topic of discussion is emotionally charged. This could include conversations around parenting, politics, health care and choices, end-of-life decisions, religion, finances, morality, education, legislation . . . you get the idea. We have more than enough scenarios in which we might clash. However, avoiding, retaliating, or shutting down difficult conversations and the people you disagree with actually causes you more harm than you realize. It stunts your spiritual growth, inhibits your emotional maturity, limits your pool of potential relationships, and may keep you in a place of loneliness and isolation. Few people want to be friends with a person who is always right.

Navigating difficult conversations isn't easy. If you feel overwhelmed by or resistant to the idea, I get it. I would rather avoid conflict and tension at all costs. But we have a Jesus who, rather than dodging disagreements, pressed into relationships. That's the kind of person I want to be too.

If conflict makes you want to shut down, tune out, or walk away, consider these five practices that can help you love well even when you disagree.

1. *Stay grounded in your gospel identity.* When differing convictions and positions become a dividing line in our relationships, it's often a result of misplaced identity. For example, if my identity is rooted in my political party, I will struggle to connect authentically

with anyone who doesn't share my position. However, you and I are called to find our identity in the saving love and grace of Christ. He defines who we are—not our various positions and affiliations. When we remember that our foremost identity is a sinner saved by grace, we will find it is much easier to connect with other sinners saved by grace.

2. *Stay curious and ask questions.* There is a direct relationship between my emotional state and my ability to stay curious. The more charged I feel, the less I'm able to stay curious. I find that simply reminding myself to stay curious keeps my emotions in check. How did they come to that conviction? What part of their story am I not aware of? Why might they feel so passionate about their position or so threatened by mine? Staying curious is not easy, but it is possible. And sincere questions are the open door to that kind of engagement.

3. *Listen.* Listening isn't simply allowing someone to talk while you formulate your rebuttal. Listening involves your ears, your eyes, and your heart. True listening requires you to put a pause on your position and defense and instead connect with the person. It requires you to resist judgment and instead listen to the words, heart, and intent of the person speaking. It means staying in a place where you want to be in relationship more than you want to be right.

4. *Communicate empathy.* This may be obvious, but people want to feel heard, including you. Once you've listened and asked questions, find at least one

connecting point to which you can honestly say, "I can see how you would feel that way" or "I understand where you're coming from." Empathy is possible even when you disagree. And it will go a long way to bridge a divide, even if neither of you changes your position.

5. *Restate the value of the relationship.* At the end of every hard conversation—and perhaps multiple times throughout—it's critical that you remind yourself and the other person that what matters most is the relationship. This will keep you focused on the ultimate outcome you hopefully both want—a respectful, mature, thriving relationship—in spite of the potential messiness of the conversation. And if you persevere in your pursuit of this goal, you won't just save the relationship, you'll likely make it even stronger.

When you find out that someone you care about has a staunchly different opinion or belief than you, it's so much easier to write them off or build an emotional wall. But what seems easiest in the moment won't serve us or our relationships well. It's time to choose a different way, one that is more humble, curious, and compassionate.

Questions to Sit With

Ask Yourself

1. What positions, principles, and convictions most often become dividing lines in my relationships?

2. Who do I most struggle to connect with and listen to as a result of seemingly irreconcilable differences?

3. When it's easy to see the many ways we disagree, is it possible to find ways in which we are the same? Would creating space for conversation and listening help?

Ask God

1. Father, where have I grown callous to Your extravagant love and grace?

2. Where am I allowing my positions, principles, and convictions to get in the way of authentic love?

3. Who is one person I need to engage with and spend more time listening to?

20

I Thought I Was Over the Hurt

Renee Swope

I thought I was over the hurt. I was certain I had moved on, but as I slipped my thumb under the seal of an invitation to my ten-year college reunion, I realized: *I had not forgiven her.*

During our last semester at school, harsh tones and accusing anger from a friend had been more than I could handle, especially in the middle of my battle with depression. I was living with deep soul-sadness and overwhelming self-doubt I couldn't explain or escape. When a friend questioned something I'd done, it was clear she was extremely frustrated with me.

Not having the mental or emotional strength to process her criticism at the time, I had allowed her words to shove me into a pit of shame.

Ten years passed, and I was a different person in many ways. Still vulnerable to others' opinions, but by the grace of God's love and healing power along with years of counseling and medication, I had been set free from the pain of my past. Or so I thought.

Even ten years later, holding the invitation to attend an event where I'd likely see her, my heart was flooded with painful and paralyzing emotions that mirrored those I had felt the day our friendship ended.

I put the reunion invitation in a drawer and tried to ignore it for weeks. Eventually, though, I got tired of being a prisoner to my pain. I wanted freedom. The kind of freedom I'd experienced in so many ways throughout the previous decade—the freedom of forgiveness Jesus died to give to me.

With every ounce of courage I had, I returned my RSVP with a brave *yes*.

In the weeks leading up to the reunion, I spent hours reading and praying through Scriptures about forgiveness, journaling through details I could remember about what had happened, and asking Jesus to help me see things from His perspective and even from hers.

During the three-hour drive to my old college campus, I listened to worship music and messages on forgiveness and my identity in Christ. I prayed for the friend who had hurt me and asked Jesus to help me see her through His eyes of compassion and love. And I asked God to drench me with His grace and give me security in Him that could not be shaken, no matter what happened when I got there.

By the time I arrived, I actually *wanted* to find my old friend and restore our relationship. It took me by surprise at first, but I knew this was God's answer to so many prayers and the beginning of my own healing. It was such a gift to feel desire instead of dread. As I walked into the reception room and saw my old friend, grace and healing came. I went over to say hello and chatted for a few minutes, and then I brought up what had happened. We talked and ended up both apologizing for hurting each other. We hugged, and in the midst of it all, Jesus did something I never could have done on my own.

Come Sit with Me and Learn Together

That day felt like a miracle, and it was—a miracle begun years earlier when Jesus extended His grace to us on the cross. With perfect love He gave up His life for imperfect people. In doing so, He showed us what it looks like to forgive: It's being "humble and gentle," and "patient, bearing with one another in love" (Eph. 4:2). It's being "kind and compassionate to one another, forgiving each other, just as in Christ God forgave [us]" (4:32).

Have you got a conflict that still needs to be resolved? Or a hurt that has never been forgiven? When you think about it today, what emotions does it stir up? Do you feel the same anger or hurt you felt when it first happened? Does it feel easier to keep your distance from that person and act like it never happened?

When we've been hurt by someone's words or actions, forgiveness is never easy. A lot of times we are afraid to forgive because it might open us up to being hurt again. Other times we hesitate to ask for forgiveness because we fear the other person might think we are the only one in the wrong and they don't need to change at all. Many times we're afraid that if we bring up past wounds with them, we'll unearth bitterness we don't want to deal with.

Although you can't go back and change the circumstances or conflicts that have hurt you, you can ask Jesus to change the impact they have on you. Take some time and ask the Lord to show you if there are unresolved conflicts He wants you to forgive. Ask Him if there are any miscommunications He wants you to work through with Him or to clear up with the other person. The key is to remember that you don't go through this process alone—the Holy Spirit is in you! He is ready and willing to bring the full wisdom of God and the healing power of Christ into your heart as you process the past and seek His guidance in moving forward.

Forgiveness is never easy. It's some of the most excruciating faith work we will ever do. But we can do it because Jesus did the greatest work of all on Calvary, paying the penalty for our sins so we could be fully forgiven and live fully free. Christ in us enables us to give others what we've been given as deeply loved, chosen, secure children of God. It's His forgiveness that sets us free so we can forgive ourselves and others.

Every wound from our past is safe in Jesus's hands. And every hope for tomorrow is possible because of what Christ has already done. What we do with His grace and mercy makes all the difference.

Questions to Sit With

Ask Yourself

1. Is there someone in my life who has hurt or betrayed me that I've never forgiven?

2. What steps can I take to forgive them and release myself from the tangled emotions of bitterness and woundedness?

3. How has unforgiveness hindered my healing and kept me from becoming secure in who I am in Christ and what I have to offer in relationships?

Ask God

1. Lord, reveal any hurt, resentment, unforgiveness, or bitterness that hinders my relationship with You, with myself, or with others in my life.

2. Jesus, show me if I am withholding from others the grace and mercy You have extended to me.

3. What do I need to do to release the hurt so I can find complete healing and wholeness in Your love?

21

How to Stop Running from Someone's Hard Places

Jen Schmidt

A my clutched the teacup, her fingers intertwined, tears streaming down her face as she grieved on the anniversary of her son's death. It had been one year—365 days, and she had counted every single one. The air hung heavy around us, a silent vapor settling. Everything in me wanted to fill the quiet with sound—with words, with wisdom, with Bible verses. Anything that might fill this cavernous void of deafening silence. I wanted to offer something grandiose, but I'd learned through decades of hard-fought and often-lost lessons that my friend's deep ache couldn't be fixed with my words. What she felt could only be fully mended by the Master Healer.

Wailing, she stumbled to her bed and curled up in the fetal position. I felt awkward, anguished, and uncomfortable. You see, Amy is the one others go to in crisis. She's strong—a helper, a problem solver, a calming presence amid trouble. Friends have described me the same way—a steady constant in a sea of tumultuous emotions. But in this moment I was tossing and turning with no life raft in sight.

Not knowing what to do or how to help, I simply joined her on the bed. I didn't overthink it or create a myriad of scenarios in my head. Whatever comfort I could offer wasn't enough to fix anything. But still I put my arms around her and whispered soft muttering cries to Jesus until her sobs subsided.

It took a very long while. And in those hours, a revelation hit me: I'd never come so close to another person's grief like that. When the breath of despair wraps around you, painfully sacred moments move relationships to heightened awareness. These moments are scarce not because moments of pain are few and far between. Sitting with someone in their grief—whether it's due to a death, depression, disease, disability, infertility, trauma, unemployment, or any number of heartaches—is rare only because we would rather rush through it and run from their reality.

For years I've been a runner. Not the long-distance kind where I'm building needed strength and stamina, but the kind where I sidestep the pain of others.

I'd slide in near enough to feel it, but as soon as their suffering hit too close to home, I'd hurry out, leaving my calling card to make sure they knew I'd been there. I'd drop the casserole and run. I'd write the card, run to the mailbox, and cross that off my list. I'd send the text and tell myself that was enough.

My first sprint occurred as a young mom. In my weekly small group Bible study, three of us gave birth to our first baby boys within one month of each other. You can imagine how that bonded us. We shared the late-night, lack-of-sleep, breast-milk-leaking-all-over kind of stories that come with the camaraderie of bleary-eyed motherhood. Ten months later, Kathy's son was diagnosed with childhood cancer. I made the obligatory meal, which is a very real and tangible need and is always the first thing I think of. But pregnant with our second child and preparing to have two kids nineteen months and under, I got busy, sidetracked—or at least that's the excuse I clung to.

When our second son was born with a congenital birth disease and was scheduled for surgery at the children's hospital, his room was directly above the room of Kathy's son, so I went to visit them. I'll never forget walking into that room. He'd already been there for a month, with no improvement in sight. The shades were pulled back, and moisture settled on my skin from too many people camped out in a closet-sized space. I can still smell the disinfectant that the hospital used in their attempt to mask the end-of-life scent.

Weeks later, our son lived, but my friend's precious baby died. I sang at his funeral. I'm glad I showed up in that hard moment, but I'm sad to say that I didn't stick around in the weeks and months after the service. I sprinted. I couldn't reconcile why our son lived and Kathy's died. I assumed it would be too hard for her to see me. I told myself I was being sensitive to her needs, but honestly, I was avoiding the discomfort of hard places.

Four months after the funeral our family moved a thousand miles away and I completely lost touch with Kathy. When I think back on that challenging year, I often wish I could have a do-over.

And in a way, I have. Because now, decades later, I've stopped running.

Lying there on the bed with Amy, clutching tissues like my childhood blankie, I looked her straight in the eyes as her sobbing subsided. "It's been one year since his death and I still don't have the right words to say. I still can't comprehend what you're going through, and I don't always know how to act, but I'm here for you. To be your person."

I blubbered through an awkward laugh-cry as I patted the bed and declared, "Or I can lie here and spoon with you." She chuckled too. "As much as I tell myself I want to relate to your anguish as a good friend, I know that I really can't. To be able to relate would mean my family going through a similar devastation. So I'm never going to completely understand, but I'm here for you for the long haul."

A year of walking through the darkest times together gave me permission to bare my heart. A year of storming the gates of heaven for my friend, knowing the devil would be on the prowl when she was at her lowest. A year of bringing food and sharing meals because her family needs sustenance and often won't eat. A year of writing Bible verses on note cards for her to read during months of insomnia. A year of texting random and wacky words just to make her smile.

"Thank you for being honest, Jen," she said. "You are one of the few safe people in my circle these days, and I know I'm no longer that fun person you once knew. I know people don't wake up and say, 'Oh, I want to hang out with Amy today.' I want to be my old fun self, but I can't make it so, and people are tired of being around me. They need me to move on and get on with a normal life, but nothing feels normal anymore. I don't know how to get back to normal, because the old normal ceased to exist."

Every word she said was true, but I'm done running.

Come Sit with Me and Learn Together

I wish I could say that I get this right all the time. I definitely don't. But when it comes to loving others as Jesus loves me, I've learned the hard way that truly leaning into kingdom transformation means I need to sit and "mourn with those who mourn" (Rom. 12:15).

Full disclosure: writing on this topic takes everything out of me. I am a full-blown Pollyanna. I nearly always see the leaking, empty cup as one that overflows, and even if it doesn't, I find ways to beautify it with fluorescent pink duct tape.

So when Romans 12:15 commands, "Rejoice with those who rejoice; weep with those who weep" (CSB), I find the first part easy to do. It's who I am to celebrate and rejoice and make sweet lemonade out of sour lemons. But to actually enter into another's sorrow and intentionally take part of their affliction and burden on myself? It's soul sucking. In fact, the Greek word translated as "weep" is *klaio*, which means "to sob or wail aloud." In the Jen paraphrase, this means we give up control, check our platitudes, dignity, and well-applied mascara at the door, and be available to fully invest in the hard work of mourning alongside others. We need to show up for them in their pain, even when it feels like more than we are capable of.

In Isaiah 53, which prophesies of Christ, we're told, "He was despised and rejected by men, a man of sorrows and acquainted with grief; and as one from whom men hide their faces he was despised, and we esteemed him not" (v. 3 ESV). Every morning I pray to be transformed more into the image

159

of God—*imago Dei*. But do I truly mean that? Not once have I asked to be despised and rejected by friends or to become more acquainted with grief like Jesus was. That's never been a goal of mine. Yet, as we grow into mature followers of Christ who desire to be refined and changed into His likeness, our willingness to walk alongside those who grieve is a clear indication that the resurrected life of Christ and the fruit of the Holy Spirit are flowing through all aspects of our lives, not just the areas we choose.

In the middle of writing this chapter, I brought a meal to a friend. Her mother is in hospice care at their home, and when I arrived, my friend asked if I wanted to see her. I silently screamed, *No! Absolutely not. Why would you even ask?* I'm embarrassed to admit that I stammered excuses: "Oh, she won't remember me. She doesn't really know me, so I'd hate to make her more tired." UGH! I'm the Bible teacher writing about sitting with others in their grief. I thought I was done running.

Instantly, I could see disappointment wash over my friend's face. Instantly, I could feel the Spirit stirring my heart toward change.

"Well, if you think she'd enjoy that, it would be my honor," I told my friend. So, off I went to visit with a precious woman who was down to just fifty-five pounds and had been given one week until she would be reunited with her Savior.

And I almost made it about me.

But today is a new day full of fresh mercies. I won't let false guilt or condemnation invade my heart, and I hope you'll choose to turn those unwelcome guests away if they come knocking at the door of your heart too. Instead, let's allow the continual stirring of the Holy Spirit to convict us in new ways, and let's partner with Him in bearing witness to others' pain.

This is hard and holy work—the good, bad, and ugly all intertwining to provide a framework for transformation. There is no quick fix, no easy three-step tutorial for leaning into hard places. But the awkward, uncomfortable learning curve we each must face is worth it. It's always worth it.

God promises to work all things for the good of those who love Him (Rom. 8:28). He's the God who turns beauty into ashes and promises to redeem all things. Those aren't words I've said to my friend Amy yet, just a year after the loss of her son. It often takes time before a person's heart is ready to see and receive God's goodness through tragedy and hardship. Amy knows God is working even through her unimaginable loss, but that's not the encouragement I offer her.

The most important gift I've been able to give her is the ministry of my presence. She's needed a listening ear, someone to whom she can vent and be angry and scream and ask why this happened. She's needed a tender heart, someone to receive her without judgment or quick fixes and to understand that the most important thing is being fully engaged in our time together.

That's a gift we can all give. To stop running. To lean into someone's grief. To take their hand and help them lean into Jesus—the ministry of our presence inviting the ministry of His.

Questions to Sit With

Ask Yourself

1. What does it look like to put my comfort and personal happiness aside to minister to someone else?
2. How willing am I to enter into someone's pain by sitting with them in untold grief even though words fail me?
3. What can I do this week to create margin and come alongside someone else?

Ask God

1. Lord, is there selfishness in my own heart that keeps me from reaching out? Please reveal it to me.
2. Holy Spirit, open my eyes to one person in my circle of influence that needs Your healing touch. Who do You want me to commit to for the long haul?
3. Lord, loving others is a long, challenging road. What does it look like to receive Your strength and perseverance to stay when everything in me wants to run?

22

Learning to Disagree While Still Honoring My Parents

Dorina Lazo Gilmore-Young

In March 2020, the world shut down. We did not know what a global pandemic would entail or how long it would last, but suddenly we were all in the thick of it. Where I live in California, we were instructed to shelter at home. People went out for groceries, toiletries, and gas, but that was about it. Gatherings were canceled. Sports were canceled. Broadway was canceled. School, life group, Bible study group, and work-related meetings were moved to Zoom and other online forums. Weeks gave way to grueling months of time spent separated from our people, churches, and workplaces. You probably have your own story of what living through that season was like.

During the pandemic, God showed me that one of the most powerful ways I could offer hospitality in this crisis was to invite my parents to shelter at home *with* us. Both of them are retired, and I quickly recognized that they were struggling with the frustration and loneliness of being isolated. We all were. As a family, we decided we wanted to provide a place of respite and connection for them. My husband and I talked it over and decided to limit our interaction with other people to protect my parents. They stayed with us most weekends and some weeknights too.

Admittedly, this was more of a challenge than I expected. I was suddenly thrust into a game of tug-of-war between my roles. I felt jerked back and forth between being a wife, a mother, a daughter, and the woman of the house. At times, this tug-of-war felt overwhelming and depleting. I was trying to parent my own three daughters and also honor my parents, whose values sometimes conflicted with ours, all under the same roof.

We all had to recalibrate.

I love my parents dearly and have maintained a good relationship with them over my four decades of life. However, it was different having them live with us. We had to sort out our personality differences and daily family rhythms.

My mom is a helper in the truest sense of the word. She delights in making meals for people, tutoring students in academics, and helping friends when they are sick. She's tender and giving and sometimes runs herself ragged serving others. She's passionate about certain causes, especially defending the most vulnerable.

My dad, on the other hand, is a challenger. He thrives by taking on challenges himself and also challenging others in conversation. He's wired for productivity. He loves to accomplish things and check boxes. He prides himself on staying up on the latest news and politics and doesn't shy away from hard conversations.

I know I have taken on qualities, passions, and mannerisms from each of my parents. I have also come to recognize that God uniquely created me as distinct and gifted in different ways from my parents. I'm a glass-half-full enthusiast who always loves to share what I'm learning. I'm a creative who enjoys connecting with God through nature, food, and storytelling. I avoid conflict as much as possible.

Sometimes these personality differences, plus the personalities of my husband and three daughters, meant we were all bumping up against one another while living in the same house. Sometimes I had to give my girls and myself permission for a time-out, not because we had a big blowup but because sometimes you just need time and space to recalibrate. I'd retreat to my bedroom to read a book or take a few extra yoga breaths.

Prior to the pandemic, my family had cultivated a rhythm of rest on the weekends, especially on Sundays. We attend church in the morning and then come home for a large meal—just the five of us or with other families from our life group. We love lingering around the table. I try to keep my computer closed and leave my phone on the charger in my bedroom to take a break from the beck and call of social media and emails. Everyone also knows that later in the afternoon it's nap time at our house.

My husband, Shawn, is an especially big proponent of naps. He rises before dawn on most weekdays to exercise and start work. Weekends are his time to catch up on much-needed physical rest. When we got married, I fell into a similar rhythm. We urge our daughters to embrace Sabbath rest too. They might not sleep on Sunday afternoons, but they are encouraged to read a book, do an art project, or listen to music quietly in their rooms while Mama and Daddy catch some extra Z's.

However, when my parents arrived during the pandemic, they were not ready to rest. Both are high achievers and like to stay active. My mom brought a heaping stack of cookbooks, craft projects, workout clothes, and puzzles to "keep busy" at our house. My dad was glued to his phone, scrolling news apps and texting friends. Neither was used to napping or taking time to be quiet on Sunday afternoons.

I quickly slipped into the familiar groove of my "hostess with the mostest" role as I often do when people are in my home, cooking up elaborate meals and bustling about to make sure everyone is well-nourished and happy. After a short time I began to feel exhausted and resentful. I was forfeiting my own rest and found myself being snappy and argumentative with my family.

There was an added layer of challenge as the hair-dryer-hot days of summer gave way to the fiery fall of 2020—an election year. My dad and I don't always see eye to eye on politics and partisanship. He wanted to talk about the election, the candidates, and the most divisive issues. I longed for a break from it all and wanted to protect my children from the constant barrage of daily headlines. All of our anxiety and grief bubbled at the surface like a volcano ready to explode.

I'm not proud to say I snapped more than once. The words that came out of my mouth were not always kind and compassionate. I was stretched thin in a lot of ways—working from home, helping my kids with their schooling, the multiplied effort of doing regular things like grocery shopping, and the daily decision fatigue during the pandemic.

In that season I had to learn how to draw some relational boundaries. My parents and I agreed to disagree on some things. We decided to put away our phones, turn off the news, and concentrate more on quality time together on the weekends. Mom and Dad learned to respect our nap time—they even joined in once in a while or took that time to stroll through our neighborhood. Over the year, I started to see transformation happen in all of us.

Come Sit with Me and Learn Together

Perhaps you've experienced something similar. Do you have that one friend who rubs you the wrong way whenever a certain subject comes up in conversation? Do you have a family member who is wired differently from you? Is it difficult to sit down at the table with someone in your life who always seems to have a different opinion? For some of us, the default may be to run away from the tension or to bury our feelings. But maybe God is calling us to stay, to work through our frustrations, and to learn to set healthy boundaries. Maybe this is the most generous thing we can offer ourselves and one another.

I know I'm still a work in progress in this area. One thing that has helped me is regularly going to Scripture for guidance and discernment when frustration flares. One of the passages I now run to in the heat of the moment is James 1:19–20: "My dear brothers and sisters, take note of this: Everyone should be quick to listen, slow to speak and slow to become angry, because human anger does not produce the righteousness that God desires."

Jesus's brother James was writing to Jewish Christians about practical ways they should live out their faith. James was not afraid to get up into people's business. In this section of the letter, he addresses speech and unrestrained anger. James uses a phrase of endearment—"my dear brothers and sisters"—to indicate a loving tone, not one of judgment. Then he goes on to give what seem like simple instructions: be quick to listen, slow to speak, and slow to become angry.

Easier said than done.

I'm learning to repeat these instructions to myself and then apply them to my situation. Often our default when we are frustrated or angry with someone is to become defensive or lash out. Instead I ask myself, What would it look like to listen well in this situation?

Listening well is knowing there is "a time to be silent and a time to speak" (Eccles. 3:7). Listening well is hearing not just with my ears but also with my eyes, heart, and body language. If I want to listen well, I have to deliberately turn toward a person with curiosity and compassion. Sometimes we can change the trajectory of a conversation simply by asking questions instead of answering with a retort. I learned to ask my dad questions like "Where did you hear that?" or "Why do you feel that way?"

Proverbs 15:18 reminds us, "A hot-tempered person stirs up conflict, but the one who is patient calms a quarrel." I find myself centering on the word "calms." I long to be the person who brings calm to a situation, not someone who stirs up tension. I want my words to be soothing, not seething. Of course, I can't bootstrap my way there. Only the Holy Spirit can help us move away from our fight-or-flight default and into that place of patience and peace.

God has also shown me the importance of setting boundaries. Dr. Henry Cloud and Dr. John Townsend unpack this in their book *Boundaries*. When we have poor boundaries, we struggle with saying no to the pressures, demands, or expectations of others. Living without healthy boundaries leads to living in fear that saying no to someone will harm the relationship, so we passively comply but inwardly resent.[1]

As a mother of three daughters, I believe it's important for me to model healthy boundaries. Setting good boundaries means identifying and communicating what I can handle or how much time I can invest in something or someone. Sometimes it means graciously saying no to a commitment or invitation. While my parents lived with us during the pandemic, setting boundaries meant physically removing myself from a situation or carving out emotional space before returning to a heavy conversation. It meant protecting my family's rhythms of rest.

Jesus is our greatest model for healthy relational boundaries. He often took time away to rest, pray, and be in communion with the Father. He didn't succumb to arguing or reply to His adversaries with sarcasm. At the same time, Jesus valued each person, and we too must learn how to value one another. Exodus 20:12 instructs, "Honor your father and your mother." For me this means speaking to my parents with a tone of respect and grace even if I hold a different political view or a news story hits me a different way.

1. Henry Cloud and John Townsend, *Boundaries* (Grand Rapids: Zondervan, 1992), 34.

By the power of the Holy Spirit, I can set and live within healthy boundaries for myself and for my family while still loving and honoring my parents. It's not easy, but it is possible. For me and for you.

*   *   *

We're back in the kitchen, the heart of our home. The familiar fragrances of garlic, oregano, and basil permeate the air. My daughters gather at the stove and take turns using a wooden spoon to swirl the ruby red tomato sauce and meatballs in the big pot. "Be careful with my meatballs," Nana Maria chides playfully. "You don't want to break any of them up."

My mama, affectionately called Nana, stands at our kitchen island with my youngest daughter, stuffing jumbo pasta shells with spoonfuls of cream cheese, spinach, and meat filling. My dad butters thick slices of garlic bread. My husband is at the sink, trying to get ahead of the train of dirty dishes.

We are all in the kitchen, moving through a cacophony of clinking dishes, laughter, singing, colorful ingredients, and inviting aromas. Eating and resting together with my parents has now become a Sunday tradition. We've learned to value one another's company even more. I deepened my trust in my parents and learned to appreciate their personalities and idiosyncrasies in new ways. Now we *look forward* to our time together every week. The pandemic pushed us to embrace our differences and treasure what we have in common.

Questions to Sit With

Ask Yourself

1. Which relationship in my life feels difficult right now?
2. In what areas might I be serving others or compliant yet resentful?
3. What does it look like to disagree with someone but still treat them with respect?

Ask God

1. Lord, in what areas do I need to set healthy boundaries?
2. Holy Spirit, show me how to be quick to listen, slow to speak, and slow to become angry. What do You want to say or do in my strained relationships? I surrender my pride and frustration to You.
3. How do You want me to value family relationships and friendships?

23

Love Your Friends and Let Them Go

Rachel Marie Kang

It's my first day at a new school and I'm nervous with fifth-grade fear and dread. I sit down at the first empty desk I find, then I wait and watch and wonder. I ask myself, *Which one?* Which one is for me? Which of these students will welcome me in? Which one will invite me into their circle? Which one will call me friend?

Then I see her. A girl with brown hair and brown eyes, smiling wide and seeming kind. I watch as she walks into the classroom, and I imagine us sharing pencils and laughing loud in the cafeteria and all the ways we will become good friends. This is all happening in my head at the same time the brown-haired girl begins to make her way to the teacher. She whispers loud enough for me—for everyone—to hear her say that some new girl in a yellow shirt and black overalls is sitting at her desk and can't the new girl just find another seat to sit at, *please*?

And, surprise, it's me. I'm the new girl, and it's my hand-me-down yellow shirt and black overalls, and those are my cheeks washing white with embarrassment as blood flushes fast from my face, and there goes the daydream in my head fading dim and dark, because it is only my first day here and already I just want to go back to my old friends at my old school.

And it turns out that this is not just one memory I have, but it's the overarching theme of my life. I am the girl who always moved when it mattered most, the girl whose roots spread wide but never deep.

The good news in all of this is that the brown-eyed girl and I, along with a few others I came to know and call my own, eventually did become good friends. And the group of us played softball together, went shopping together, sat at long lunch tables together talking about the boys we liked. But it wouldn't be long before I'd move again, for the third time in about three years, *thank you very much*. And this is where the story still stings, where it's hard and where my heart holds the kind of hurt that plays hide and seek— a haunting that disappears and then reappears, just like that.

I'm in middle school and it's my birthday and I'm mopey from still missing my old friends, when suddenly the doorbell rings. It's a surprise, and there stand my friends, greeting me for a sleepover. They come in, the whole group of them, like we're all back in fifth grade again, with gifts to give and secrets to spill. And the next day, before their long drive back to the town where I used to live, all of us walk to the corner convenience store and buy soda in glass bottles to pretend that we are intoxicated, guzzling colas like we are drunk, thinking we are invincible and indestructible and older than we really are.

After everyone leaves, I save their bottles. I keep them in my closet for months, calling them keepsakes I'll cherish forever. But in time I realize that, even though I can hold on to those bottles, I cannot hold on to these friendships. Because before I know it, the meetups happen less and less, as do the invitations, instant messenger conversations, and text messages to my prepaid Nokia. The physical and figurative distance between us is the slowest burn as six friendships dissipate one by one, and I'm left feeling like that lonely little girl in hand-me-down overalls all over again.

Come Sit with Me and Learn Together

One of the hardest parts about moving or growing up or changing is learning that inevitably there will come a time when you'll walk that line of losing and letting go of friends you love. It's realizing how you cannot always hold on to the people and places that have shaped who you've become. It's seeing that there is a tightrope, a tension that makes you want to cling to the past while requiring you to hesitantly inch forward and clench tightly to the present.

I had to learn to let my old friends go, even though I still loved them. I had to learn to let the friendships go, both the fellowship and the familiarity of them—that sense of returning to someone because you already know them and they already know you. Learning can be painful. It *is* painful. I had to do the hard work of opening my bottled-up heart and placing it into the present. I had to learn the kind of letting go that honestly acknowledges when the distance is too far and when it's okay to allow a friendship to fade into a forever kind of goodbye.

What's wild about all of this is that it isn't just a fifth-grade fear and dread. It's a reality for every one of us, no matter the season we find ourselves in. It's hard and it's nuanced and there are layers and complications beyond what we can even imagine. But we are not alone in these moments of letting go. We are held and we are known, and there is hope and help for every healing heart.

The hope and help is *Jesus*. Jesus knew how to let go of the friends He loved. When His time on earth was nearing its end, He told His friends that He would be leaving, but He also told them that the Father would never let them go. As His life changed, as He returned to the Father, He promised His friends that the Spirit of truth would attend to them and be present in His absence: "And I will ask the Father, and he will give you another advocate to help you and be with you forever—the Spirit of truth" (John 14:16–17). He knew how and when and why to let go. And He didn't do it merely because of *time*; He did it because of *truth*.

And the truth is that Jesus trusted the Father's love for His friends. He trusted that the Father would fulfill all that He promised to them. He didn't try to cling to them out of control or to prove He cared for them. He trusted that, even in His absence, the Father would still be at work in and through the lives of the ones He loved, fiercely leading them but also fully loving them.

The hard but holy thing about all of this is that not one of us—no matter how good of a friend we are or how much we care—can be infinitely present everywhere at the same time.

We cannot be infinitely present through texting, through FaceTime, through Instagram. We cannot split ourselves to be with all people in all places at all times. Sometimes I ache over the reality of my limitedness. I want to be all places at all times so my friendships never fracture or falter or fade away. But God gives limits for our good and His glory, because our doing and our being will always fall short of what we want or what others need. Our intentions will always dim in the light of the Father's limitless love. He is the one who gets to shine for all He is and does.

So when we're called—or forced—to move forward, may we remember the one who holds our friends and our future. May we believe in the Father who empowered Jesus to leave the ones He loved. Not because He didn't love them. Not because He needed or wanted out. Instead, He came to trust the quiet voice that was leading Him to a new place and a new purpose.

And this is not to promise that the ache of loss will ever leave you. This is not to say that the road won't feel like it is filled with wreckage and ruin. But by the Father's love we can heal. And by the Spirit's truth we'll find our help. And by Jesus's example we can live with hope, thanking the Father for the gift of friendship and the truth that at the end of all our loving and letting go, He will always welcome us into His circle. He will always call us friends.

Questions to Sit With

Ask Yourself

1. Thinking back to my earliest childhood memories of friendship: What is one good memory I have of loving a friend? What is one painful memory I have of letting go of a friend?

2. What is the connection between these memories and how I approach friendships today?

3. What is one word or phrase that describes what I have learned from friendships I've had to let go of? (Examples: trusting God, courage, adaptability, solitude)

Ask God

1. God, where have You been a friend to me?

2. God, am I carrying any guilt from friendships I've had to let go of? Please show me and help me to release those feelings of guilt.

3. God, what does it look like to trust You in my friendships with others and in my friendship with You?

24

When to Offer Your Presence over Positivity

Joy Groblebe

My sweet friend Michele had cancer. Again.

And not the easy "we'll take it out and you'll be fine" kind of cancer . . . if there even is such a thing. She had cancer of the tongue—again—and it was bad. Really bad.

After an excruciating surgery where the surgeons had removed a third of her tongue and used skin from her arm to create a new tongue and skin from her leg to replace the skin on her arm (yes, it was as major and awful as it sounds), she was recovering. Slowly.

Michele was about five months postsurgery, and we were at a conference together in the mountains of Colorado. It was there, in a hotel hallway, that I learned the value of "come sit with me."

My whole life I've been told that I'm an optimist. My first name is Joy, so I guess it kind of comes with the territory. It's hard to be named Joy and be a negative person. Think of the character Joy from the movie *Inside Out* and, well, that's a rather good representation of me.

My mom also thrives on optimism and positivity. As the story goes, when she was about sixteen years old, she just decided that she was always going to find the best in everything. She would not dwell on the negative but always look for the positive. She would find a bright light in everything because, as she'd say, "there is always one there if you look hard enough." And if you've ever met my mom in real life, you would know that she lives this out day after day after day.

So when problems come and bad things happen, my tendency is to follow in my mom's footsteps and look for the bright spot—and then figure out how to fix the junk. I can't help but look for the positive and determinedly move forward. The way I see it, there's no need to sit in the negative; just find the positive and move on. Quickly. Why sit in deep, dark holes or painful places when you can just push through and get to the positive?

As I would soon learn, this posture of untiring positivity wasn't always shared, nor was it always helpful.

The conference Michele and I were at was an annual event. We were back helping run it that year, and the event marked one of Michele's first work engagements since her most recent surgery. We had worked together for years, and this conference used to be our normal. We would go fourteen to sixteen hours a day for five days straight. It was exhilarating and rewarding, a time we always looked forward to. But now, after surgery, after multiple cancers, nothing was normal. Michele was exhausted. She made it through each day, but nothing was easy. She had no sense of taste. Eating was excruciating. Even talking was difficult—and this was a conference for speakers.

A few days into the week, we were walking down the hall back to our hotel room after a very long day. Michele was sharing with me some things that had happened and how she was feeling. It had been a really hard day, the work was overwhelming, and even the simplest things were difficult. Her body was completely drained and her pain was immense.

I immediately went into full-on Joy mode. I did my thing. I started encouraging her. Started telling her how far she'd come. How strong she was. How she was going to beat this thing—she was practically through it! I explained to her that by focusing on the future and all the good things God had planned for her, the bad parts would lessen and she would see the positive in all her progress.

I was inspiring her, uplifting her, pushing her forward, and "helping" her in her time of need.

Michele listened quietly, and then she looked at me and told me to stop. With a raised voice, she let me know that she didn't want to hear about the good or how strong she was. She didn't need me to push her forward, because the mere thought of forward was overwhelming—her pain was too great. She couldn't focus on the future and the plans God had for her long life, because it was all she could do to just get through the next few hours, let alone the next week or the next month. Thinking about the years ahead was impossible. In that moment she did not need me to encourage her or help her find the bright side. I wasn't helping. I was just making things worse.

She did not need me to fix anything. She just needed me to sit with her.

Michele explained that she was in a deep, dark hole of pain and healing and hard, and she just needed me to be with her there. To sit with her in the deep, dark pit. To sit with her in her pain. To sit with her in the middle of a very difficult, messy situation. To not fix anything, to not find the good, to not push through. To just sit with her in the pain.

Come Sit with Me and Learn Together

In Judaism there is a grieving ritual known as shiva (or "sitting shiva" in English), which is the weeklong mourning period after burial observed by first-degree relatives (parents, siblings, spouses, and children) of the person who has died. After the initial anguish and grief of losing their loved one, shiva creates an environment of comfort and community for the mourners. The immediate family stays together at home while friends and extended relatives visit to offer their condolences and support. Sitting shiva provides a structure for the grief process and creates an expected rhythm for a community to come alongside those who have lost a loved one.[1]

In the book of Job, as Job is mourning the loss of all his children and his own physical health, three friends come to sit with him: "Then they sat on the ground with him for seven days and nights. No one said a word to Job, for they saw that his suffering was too great for words" (2:13 NLT). Job's friends sat shiva with him.

Michele needed me to sit shiva with her. Not to fix things. Not to prod her forward. Just to sit with her. To let her

1. Wikipedia, s.v. "Shiva (Judaism)," last edited December 22, 2021, https://en.wikipedia.org/wiki/Shiva_(Judaism).

express her sorrow, to bear witness to the tremendous loss she'd experienced, and to make space for her to ride out her pain in her own way and on her own schedule. In the fashion of ancient Jewish mourners, when Michele was ready, she would slowly reenter society, push through, and find hope in the future. But for now she just needed me to sit with her.

Like me, maybe you're a glass-half-full kind of person, and staying in a place of pain—for yourself or with someone else—does not come naturally. Or maybe you've endured so much through your own hardships and trauma that you don't feel like you have the capacity to empathize with or hold space for a friend's sorrow. Either way, the thing we can learn from the practice of shiva is that no personality test or checklist of circumstances is required for you to climb into someone's dark hole of mourning.

We are all qualified to sit. To be quiet. To say nothing. To not fix.

Put your hand over your mouth if you need to. Bring a box of tissues to share. You don't have to feel comfortable. Showing up to sit shiva with someone who is grieving doesn't have to be easy or feel natural. You can just come.

It reminds me of the story of Lazarus in John 11. When Jesus finally arrived on the scene after Lazarus died, He encountered His two distraught friends, Martha and Mary, the sisters of Lazarus. If anyone was qualified to step in as a cheerleader and fixer and look-for-the-bright-spot encourager, it was Jesus! But what did Jesus do?

When Jesus saw [Mary] weeping and saw the other people wailing with her, a deep anger welled up within him, and he was deeply troubled. "Where have you put him?" he asked them. They told him, "Lord, come and see." Then Jesus wept. The people who were standing nearby said, "See how much he loved him!" (John 11:33–36 NLT)

When Jesus saw Mary weeping, He wept. He didn't push her to the tomb where Lazarus would ultimately be brought back to life. He didn't prod her to be thankful for what was or counsel her to think positively about what was yet to come. Jesus simply acknowledged Mary's deep sorrow with His own genuine tears.

This is the high calling, the deep ache, the gift of learning to come sit.

Putting aside my optimistic tendencies was the most unnatural thing for me when I saw my friend hurting. But Michele didn't need me to fix her. She needed me to just be. To be right there. To be willing to sit in the pain with her. It wasn't my natural bent, but it was the best thing for her. It was the best thing for our friendship.

I learned so much from this experience, and I have relived it a hundred times since then. I learned that there is value in patience, in sitting in the mess, in feeling it all—both for others and even for myself. I don't have to rush through to find the good. I can just sit for a while.

And here's the thing: God is right there too. He's right there in the deep, dark pit of sadness, of grief, of pain. He will never leave you. He will sit shiva with you, and when you are ready, He will walk with you to slowly reenter society and discover the good plans He has for your life. Plans to give you hope and purpose. Plans to prosper you and to give you a future and peace.

But some days people just aren't ready for tomorrow's plans. They just need a friend, a sister, a daughter, a wife, a mother, a mentor, a fellow mourner to climb in the dark hole with them.

Just being together is enough.

Questions to Sit With

Ask Yourself

1. When someone I love is going through a painful season, what is my natural response?
2. Who in my life might need me to crawl into the hole with them and just sit?
3. What pain in my own life am I unwilling to sit with?

Ask God

1. How do You want me to show Your love for someone who is hurting today?
2. Why do You value compassion, mourning, silence, and community?
3. From Jesus's response to Mary's pain, what do You want me to learn about who You are and how You desire me to live?

Keeping an Open Heart after a Friendship Failure

Dawn Camp

ooking back, I can see my thirties were a whirlwind of a decade. Five of our eight children were born during those years, and I was homeschooling students from preschool to high school while toddlers and babies vied for my time and attention. I helped lead an active homeschool group and taught a geography class at our co-op. Someone in our neighborhood once told my mom that if she drove by our house at any time, day or night, the lights were always on. Our kitchen never closed, and our washer and dryer never stopped. I'm not sure how I found the time to sleep.

As crazy as things were, I had a super support system. I did life with some local ladies who had each other's backs and communicated in the day-to-day, intimate sort of way that enabled us to understand how to pray for one another and to know when we needed to jump in and lend a hand. We showed up with casseroles when one of us was sick or had a baby. We watched each other's children during doctor's appointments. We exchanged books and recipes and life hacks. We wept together at our parents' funerals. We bore one another's burdens.

I've rarely been so deeply rooted in community as I was in those days.

One day a situation arose that ultimately changed everything. The details mattered at the time, but now, nearly twenty years later, they're irrelevant. Words were spoken, decisions were made, feelings were hurt, relationships were wounded, and one family cut themselves off from contact with the rest of us. No more phone chats. No more playdates. No more connection. Nothing. Period. Fellowship with a family that had been part of my family's daily life ended suddenly, like the slamming of a door. It affected me, my children, and my immediate community.

Although I didn't realize it at the time, our season of living in that area was winding down. My mother's lengthy battle with sickness and pain was nearing its end, and the year after she died we moved eighty miles away. Over time, the other women from our community may have healed their relationships with the family who cut ties—honestly, I don't know. But I never had the chance. I never even knew if it was possible. In spite of the miles between us, I occasionally caught a glimpse of my old friend at a homeschool conference or saw her son at a track meet. But we never spoke again.

There's a reason forgiveness often feels beyond our human nature. In Ephesians 4:32 we're told, "And be kind to one another, tenderhearted, forgiving one another, even as God in Christ forgave you" (NKJV). True forgiveness requires a supernatural level of humility and a willingness to set aside all grievances. In my head I understand that I have no right to hold grudges or withhold forgiveness from anyone, considering the fact that God forgave me of a lifetime of sin and accepted His Son's sacrifice on my behalf. But in my heart, that knowledge can be hard to practice.

At the time of my friendship breakup, not only was I unsure of how to move forward, I also wasn't sure either of us was ready to set aside our feelings for the sake of repairing the friendship. I'm a peacemaker by nature, and conflict upsets me. The closer I am to a person or situation, the deeper my distress when relational feathers get ruffled and the harder I work to avoid disagreements. This is no secret to people who know me. After going through this period of intense conflict, I developed defense mechanisms to keep it from happening again. I wanted to avoid relational hurt at all costs.

When we moved to a new area where we were surrounded by new people, I wasn't as open as I used to be. I held people at arm's length and didn't let them get too close. I wanted real friendships but found it difficult to be vulnerable. Unhealed wounds can do that. Years later, I sometimes catch myself falling into this same pattern.

I wish I could share how that close but fractured friendship was restored. It's hard to leave the story unresolved. But the hard truth is that some broken relationships never heal; some friendships don't stand the test of time. That's not fun to hear if you're like me and always try to fix things. But as with many difficult life experiences, God doesn't waste our pain. God used this broken friendship to help prepare me for future relationships.

Come Sit with Me and Learn Together

Have you ever hit a relationship roadblock so large you wondered if it would be easier to break ties and walk away than do the tough work of restoration? Friendships can be downright hard sometimes. Our instinctive desire to escape pain may make running seem easier than staying. But trust me, it's not easy to sever strong emotional bonds. The same way carrying a heavy load eventually wears you down physically, heavy inner burdens take an emotional toll. Digging in out of love and refusing to give up on a friend or a friendship is hard and holy work.

Thankfully, I've experienced relationships that have overcome periods of deep hurt and differences of opinion and emerged stronger on the other side. I'll never enjoy conflict, but I've found it can be worthwhile to endure discomfort and work through differences in order to save a friendship.

The only way to protect yourself from getting hurt in friendships is to close off your heart. But closing off your heart means your relationships will remain superficial. It's true that vulnerability opens us up to deeper hurts, but it's also one of the key ingredients to having deep and meaningful friendships. And that's a God-given need that ought to surpass our desire for self-protection.

In my story of broken friendship, we all remained true to what was most important to us at the time, but we lost out on preserving a valuable piece of our community. Sure, some friendships are meant to last only for a season. Certainly there are occasions for setting relational boundaries or cutting ties if a friendship becomes toxic or the misalignment of values infringes on our mental, emotional, or spiritual health. But what if calling it quits when conflict comes calling isn't the only answer?

If you can open your heart to others while standing for truth and remaining true to yourself, you'll become the most valuable kind of friend: one who can speak the truth in love. The apostle Peter encourages us, "Above all, keep fervent in your love for one another, because love covers a multitude of sins" (1 Pet. 4:8 NASB). A fervent love doesn't give up, doesn't run when things get tough. A fervent love holds fast to the truth while giving grace, knowing that much grace is needed in return.

Speaking the truth in love can also mean knowing when to hold our tongues. My great-aunt was beloved by generations of nieces and nephews. She passed away in her nineties, unmarried and without children of her own. I used to say she liked to be the bearer of bad news because she loved to tell a story that would draw a reaction from her listeners. (There wasn't a speck of malice in her; she just liked to surprise people.) But in thinking about my sweet aunt along with my past wounds and mistakes, here's a word of caution for all of us: if you delight in delivering news that contains a bit of shock value, be careful not to share stories that have been entrusted to your ears alone.

We can unintentionally compromise the bonds of trust in a friendship when we start to care more about a crowd's reaction than a friend's heart. You may never realize the friendships that wither or the opportunities you might have had to minister to someone if they hadn't been afraid of saying too much to you, worried you might inadvertently embarrass them or break their trust. No one wants even their cleanest laundry aired to the world.

It wasn't anyone's intention, but because the situation that severed my friendship years ago was public, that exposure made healing and restoration even more difficult. Since then I've become more sensitive to the ways a person can be hurt within a friendship, and I hope to always be found trustworthy.

If you've wounded a friend or been wounded in a friendship, you may find transparency and trust hard to achieve, but in my experience the results are worth the effort. If you can be vulnerable in friendships, be a safe space for a friend to share her words or her heart, and be able to hold hard conversations in love, you'll find yourself blessed with deep friendships that stand the test of time.

Questions to Sit With

Ask Yourself

1. Am I willing to be vulnerable and open myself up to meaningful friendships, even if I might get hurt or they may not last?
2. In what situation or relationship do I need to speak the truth in love, even when it's uncomfortable?
3. Can I be trusted with my friend's secrets?

Ask God

1. Is there someone I need to forgive or apologize to in order to heal a friendship?
2. Lord, how can I show myself to be a safe place for a friend who needs a listening ear?
3. Where do I need stamina to stick with friends who need me, even when it's hard? Lord, help me persevere!

Forgiving before
an Apology

Stephanie Bryant

I remember sitting on the edge of our bed, holding our newborn daughter, crying and begging my husband not to go for another all-afternoon bike ride. I was sleep deprived. I was recovering from an emergency C-section and had a terrible case of mastitis. And I was feeling completely overwhelmed and lonely.

My husband traveled extensively for his job and was gone 90 percent of the time already. But now the 10 percent of his time spent at home was focused on training for an Ironman.

For those of you who don't know, an Ironman is the mack daddy of all triathlons. Race day consists of swimming 2.4 miles, biking 112 miles, and running 26.22 miles. It's brutal. It requires incredible determination, athletic ability, and commitment to training.

My husband had been doing triathlons for five years. I had attended races all over the United States and cheered him on. I was so proud of what he was capable of and had accomplished already.

The Ironman race was his childhood dream, and I wanted him to have this experience. But my soul was weary, my emotions were shot, and deep down I was devastated because I felt like he was choosing training for this race over me and the miracle daughter we had prayed seven years for.

My mind understood what it took to do a race like the Ironman, and I knew it had to be now or never, since it was the culmination of all of my husband's hard work. But logic and my deep need to feel loved couldn't see eye to eye, causing anger and bitterness to take root in my heart.

My husband left for his bike ride that day. We were frustrated with each other because neither of us understood what the other really needed. My pain festered into resentment toward him, and I'm sure he didn't feel supported or very loved by me either.

A few months later, my husband flew off to do the Ironman, only this time I chose to be supportive. I made a onesie for our daughter that read "Swim, Bike, Run," and we watched the race on my laptop to see him cross the finish line. This was my first step toward forgiveness.

As the years ticked by, God worked on my heart to forgive my husband for his absence during those first few months of our daughter's life. I chose to remember how he would come home from a long business trip and do the laundry, clean the house, and make dinner when I looked like a zombie mess. I chose to realize that becoming a dad isn't any easier than becoming a mom. I chose to see how patient he was toward me with all of my doubts about motherhood. I chose to realize that while his timing wasn't the best, the Ironman race was the pinnacle of his determined training and I needed to be proud of him and celebrate his achievement.

But I couldn't celebrate without first turning the situation over to the Lord. I don't remember the exact day when it happened, but the Holy Spirit was kind enough to keep nudging me toward the freedom of forgiveness. Those painful months of disappointment were tainting my view of my husband as my partner and the father of our child. I needed a new lens—the forgiveness that only God could empower me to give.

And then one day it happened. Not because I manipulated or guilted my husband into an apology, which was something I had a tendency to do, but straight out of the blue. Because God works on each of our hearts little by little and sometimes in grand gestures. I was folding towels in our laundry room when my husband came in, leaned against the counter, and asked my forgiveness for how insensitive he had been in leaving me to train and race when we had just had our daughter. Needless to say, I was stunned. He asked my forgiveness for not being there for me when I really needed him.

The floodgates opened as I cried tears of relief that he noticed and loved me enough to say he was sorry, especially years later when he might not have thought it was even necessary. I relayed my version of the story and told him why I didn't understand. He shared his feelings about that time in his life and reflected on why he was so driven. He asked me to forgive him and apologized for the pain he had caused me. He told me how thankful he was that I was such a good mom to our daughter, and he said that if he could go back in time, he wouldn't have done the race but would have stayed with us.

Still in shock, I asked him what brought about this change. Why the apology now? He said it was because of a conversation he had with a younger father who wanted to get into racing and came to him for training advice. My husband told this younger dad not to do it. That was his advice: not to train so he wouldn't miss out on what's most important and so he could be a better support to his wife.

I was so thankful for my husband's humble apology. God had revealed truth to him through his own life that he was brave enough to share not only with me but also with another family. Standing in our laundry room in that moment, I realized God had been incredibly kind to help me forgive him *before* he even apologized.

I thanked my husband for loving me and for his sincere, heartfelt apology. I told him I had already forgiven him a long time ago but that his gesture made me feel loved and helped to heal the past hurts. We hugged and then looked down to see our preschool-aged daughter watching the entire scene. My husband scooped her up in his arms and we all three embraced.

Come Sit with Me and Learn Together

When people disappoint you or even hurt you at your weakest moment, you have to choose to trust God not only with your pain but also with the person who did the damage.

Any major life moments—a new job, health issues, marriage, a new baby, divorce, a big move—can cause all kinds of stress and crisis in relationships. Some we can easily navigate and quickly solve, but some take years to unravel and deal with in a godly manner.

I've learned forgiveness is a choice, not a feeling. And if we wait until we *feel* ready to forgive or for the other person to feel bad and ask for our forgiveness, we probably won't ever live in the freedom of forgiveness.

Jesus's life shows that He forgave our sins long before we ever repented: "But God proves his own love for us in that while we were still sinners, Christ died for us" (Rom. 5:8 CSB). In the same way, God asks us to follow Jesus's example: "Let all bitterness, anger and wrath, shouting and slander be removed from you, along with all malice. And be kind and compassionate to one another, forgiving one another, just as God also forgave you in Christ" (Eph. 4:31–32 CSB). Following His example means being quick to forgive, choosing to love others no matter the offense, releasing them from the tight clutches of our need for an apology, and living in the freedom that comes from forgiveness.

After this experience with my husband, I learned that forgiving before the apology is even sweeter than waiting for the other person to ask. When we hinge our forgiveness on the moment of someone else's repentance, then—if that moment ever comes—we are more likely to have a flood of emotions in a brief instant. Unresolved bitterness and rage might take center stage as we quickly try to process the other person's apology and request for forgiveness.

Scripture never says we should let someone else's behavior dictate our timetable of forgiveness. God puts forgiveness in our court. The apostle Paul says it this way: "Make allowance for each other's faults, and forgive anyone who offends you. Remember, the Lord forgave you, so you must forgive others" (Col. 3:13 NLT).

Forgiving someone before they apologize makes true reconciliation and restoration feasible and much easier. Whether it's in the quietness of your own heart or face-to-face while leaning on the laundry room counter or sitting together at a table, forgiveness is possible. May it begin with us.

Questions to Sit With

Ask Yourself

1. Am I holding unforgiveness toward someone who has hurt me? Knowing they may or may not apologize, will I choose to forgive them anyway?

2. How would accepting the truth that people can and do change impact my relationships?

3. What part may I have played in a hurtful situation? How can I own my part and also keep praying for the person who wronged me? "Be patient in trouble, and keep on praying" (Rom. 12:12 NLT).

Ask God

1. Holy Spirit, help me choose to forgive, and remove from my heart the bitterness and anger toward the person who has wronged me.

2. God, what would true reconciliation in my hurtful relationship look like? How can we focus our hearts on You together?
3. Lord, what do You want to say to me today about forgiveness, humility, and moving forward?

final thoughts

Now's the time I wish I could invite you into my living room. I'd put a log on the fire and tell you to choose whichever spot on the couch looked coziest to you. There'd be a woven afghan if you felt like cuddling up, and of course something hot to drink. Then we would just sit. Breathe. Be. Invite Jesus into the moment with us.

When you felt ready, I'd lean in and ask to hear how the stories in this book touched your soul. Which of them do you find yourself still thinking about? What lesson did God whisper to your heart? Which words or phrases made you shake your head in disagreement? What truths were so hard to swallow that they're still stuck in your throat? Did any of it stir up hope? What prayer or perspective shift has already prompted a change in one of your relationships?

My hunch is that there's a chapter or two you'll carry with you for a long time because you saw yourself or relived a piece of your own story through those pages. Tell me that story. I'm also guessing that, like me, you encountered experiences you couldn't relate to but that made you think. You tucked a tip or a truth in your back pocket because one day you just might need it. Tell me that too.

These stories are not just meant to be read, to have you nod along or give a silent headshake or amen. These stories are meant to be a catalyst for the unfolding of your own story. Sit with what you've learned. Sit with the questions you've asked yourself and God. Keep sitting in the tension of your differences, disagreements, and discomfort.

I'm right there with you. This stuff is hard. Sometimes I'd rather run for the woods than sit in a diner booth with a person who thinks differently than I do. But I keep coming back to four words spoken through our friends in these pages: *curiosity*, *tenderness*, *time*, and *grace*.

Michele Cushatt wrote about staying curious when we disagree. Curiosity compels us to seek understanding of someone else's viewpoint rather than argue for our own opinion. Curiosity puts respect for another person above our own assumptions. Curiosity says I will listen thoughtfully even if I don't share your beliefs. Let's stay curious in our relationships.

I recall Tasha Jun's call to tenderness. The very word makes my breathing slow. Tenderness is an invitation to be gentle with ourselves and others. Tenderness acknowledges that each person carries wounds and experiences we cannot see. Tenderness doesn't rush or bully or bulldoze feelings. Tenderness makes space for what is with a quiet hope for what is to come. Let's stay tender in our friendships.

And sometimes what we need most is time. Lucretia Berry reminded us that we can't push through to healing and forgiveness. Sometimes our bitterness and desire for vengeance need time to extinguish before we're ready to let God fan a flame of compassion and forgiveness in our hearts. That's okay. Accept the gift of time. Accept the slow and purposeful way God is inviting you to understand His unconditional, unrelenting love for you. Let the assurance of His care be the loudest voice you hear. God will never get tired of sitting with you. Let's take all the time with Him that we need.

Curiosity, tenderness, and time are all arrows pointing to Patricia Raybon's reminder about grace. Indeed, God's grace is sufficient for our weakness. His grace is enough to bridge the gaps between our differences. When we focus on grace—the unearned favor of God—rather than the ways others have disappointed us, we open our hearts to the gift of sitting with friends and family we might otherwise be tempted to discount or despise. We open our lives to the gift of making pies and seeing God work miracles around Thanksgiving tables. Grace. Amazing grace. That is the thread that holds together every hard conversation, changing friendship, painful circumstance, or redeemed relationship. Let's bring grace to every bench, booth, couch, and table.

At this point I'd offer to warm up your tea or coffee (I like my hot beverages *hot*) and then ask if I could tell you just a few more things.

I want to make sure you know that the encouragement offered in this book doesn't apply to abusive relationships. If you are being verbally, emotionally, mentally, spiritually, physically, or sexually abused or exploited in any way, you do not have to embrace the discomfort your abuser is causing you. All marriages, friendships, and parent-child relationships have their challenges. But feeling the frustration of being misunderstood or having different political or religious beliefs is not the same as being abused or mistreated. As

Bonnie Gray talked about in her chapter on toxic relationships, we need to be women of discernment who learn to set healthy boundaries with toxic people so we can be available to sit with God and let Him speak into the places in our lives that need healing.

If you're not sure how to identify whether there is a toxic person in your life, consider this: recognizing a toxic person may be more about identifying how they make you feel and less about what they do or say. If you're interacting with a person who has toxic behaviors, you might

- feel confused and unsure of yourself
- leave the interaction feeling drained, angry, or full of anxiety
- feel bad about yourself in some way
- continually feel the need to help them
- notice that your boundaries aren't being respected or you're being manipulated
- experience guilt for saying "no" or feel they won't take "no" for a final answer
- feel like you're "walking on eggshells" around them
- frequently change your behavior to adapt[1]

If you are tangled in the trap of a toxic relationship, or if you're just not sure whether the angst you're feeling is a normal part of being a complicated person relating to other complicated people, please get support. Talk to a counselor

---

1. This list is taken from Kimberly Drake, "What's a Toxic Person and How to Deal with Them," PsychCentral, updated November 14, 2021, https://psychcentral .com/blog/whats-a-toxic-person-how-do-you-deal-with-one#tips-for-coping.

or therapist. Let someone sit with you and help you sort through the pain and confusion. Is God with you? Absolutely. We stand firm in the promise that says, "The LORD himself goes before you and will be with you; he will never leave you nor forsake you" (Deut. 31:8). But sometimes God also chooses to be with us through other people who are trained in helping us explore the deeply wounded places of our hearts.

Friend, you are worthy of healing. You are worthy of freedom. You are worthy of being seen and cared for. Your pain is worth someone climbing into your deep, dark hole and just being with you there. If you are in need, please call for help today.

You are so very loved. Thank you for sitting with me and the women of (in)courage through these pages.

Now may the God of all hope and healing, tenderness and curiosity, time and grace sit close with you today. May He guide your next conversation, your next question, your next point of connection. May you see Him more clearly as you sit with others.

Your sister on the journey,
Becky Keife
(in)courage community manager

questions to ask when you're sitting together

If you've learned anything through this book, we hope it's this: while it may not be easy to delight in differences, love through disagreements, or live with discomfort, it *is* possible. And it's worth it. As you navigate the hard and hope-filled relationships in your life, use this bank of questions as a resource to help you continue showing up with curiosity, tenderness, time, and grace—for others and for yourself.

Learn Their Story

1. What food reminds you of your childhood and makes you feel comforted?
2. What's something you wish people didn't assume about you?
3. What's something only people who know you well know about you?
4. When's the last time you laughed really hard?

5. What do you like to do simply for the fun of it?

6. What movie can you watch again and again and why?

7. Tell me about a memory that makes you feel safe.

8. Tell me about your favorite book.

9. Who has been an influential person in your life?

10. What makes you feel cared for?

Understand Their Perspective

1. How did you come to hold that particular belief?

2. Why is that issue so important to you?

3. What's making you come alive in this season?

4. What's causing your heart pain right now?

5. What's your favorite thing about your cultural background?

6. Is there something that would be helpful for me to understand about your story?

7. What's the greatest influence on what you believe?

8. How easy or difficult is it for you to consider opposing perspectives?

9. Are there areas of stress or hardship in your life?

10. What do you wish others understood about your perspective?

Navigate Conflict

1. What is your conflict style?

2. What kind of communication do you prefer?

3. How do you wish I would have responded?

4. Can you tell me more about what you mean by that?

5. Can I share with you how that sits with me?

6. What would it look like for us to move forward together?

7. Do you need more time to think before you respond?

8. Can I reflect what I've heard you say so far?

9. What do you hear me saying?

10. What shared goal can we agree on?

Grow Deeper Together

1. How can I love you well in this season?

2. How can I help create a place where you feel safe to share your heart?

3. What do you value most in a friendship?

4. How can I celebrate what God is doing in your life?

5. Would you like to share a significant memory about that?

6. What do you wish was different in our relationship?

7. How can we invest in our relationship in a way that feels meaningful to you?

8. Can I share with you a way I've felt wounded?

9. What is an area you would like to personally grow in?

10. How are you seeing God at work in your life?

Use this space to write down questions of your own or record questions that someone else asked that have been meaningful to you. When you feel at a crossroads with your-self, your spouse, your best friend, or your neighbor, come back to this list. Asking questions is the beginning of seeing. And we all want to be seen.

about the authors

Becky Keife is the community manager for (in)courage, a passionate speaker, and the author of *The Simple Difference: How Every Small Kindness Makes a Big Impact* and the (in)courage Bible studies *Courageous Kindness* and *Create in Me a Heart of Peace*. She and her husband live near Los Angeles where they enjoy hiking shady trails with their three spirited sons. Connect with Becky on Instagram @beckykeife or at beckykeife.com.

Lucretia Berry is the founder of Brownicity, an agency committed to making important, scholarly, informed antiracism education accessible. A former college professor, she has authored *Hues of You—An Activity Book for Learning About the Skin You Are In* and *What LIES Between Us—Fostering First Steps Toward Racial Healing*. Lucretia is married to Nathan; they have three daughters and two Aussiedoodles. Learn more from Lucretia at brownicity.com or on Instagram @lucretiaberry.

Stephanie Bryant is a cofounder of (in)courage, a social marketing and branding consultant, and a mom to a miracle. Stephanie has a podcast called *The Jesus Led Adventure* where she passionately guides her listeners to their personal promised land. Find out more about Stephanie at stephanie bryant.me and on Instagram @stephaniesbryant.

Dawn Camp shares God's gift of essential oils in her newest releases, *My Essential Oil Companion* and *It All Began in a Garden*. She is a photographer, essential oil slinger, Mom to eight, and Mimi to six. Dawn enjoys movie dates with her husband and steaming cups of Earl Grey. Visit Dawn at dawncamp.com or on social media @dawncamp.

Mary Carver writes and speaks with humor and honesty, encouraging women with truth found in unexpected places. She hosts a podcast about pop culture and faith and is the author of *Women of Courage, Journey to the Cross*, and the (in)courage Bible studies *Courageous Joy* and *Create in Me a Heart of Hope*, as well as a coauthor of *Empowered: More of Him for All of You*. Connect with Mary online at marycarver.com and on social media @marycarver.

Grace P. Cho is a Korean American writer, poet, speaker, and editor. She is a coauthor of *Empowered: More of Him for All of You* and the author of the (in)courage Bible studies *Courageous Influence* and *Create in Me a Heart of Wisdom*. Learn more at gracepcho.com and connect with her on social media @gracepcho.

Michele Cushatt is a storyteller at heart, a three-time head-and-neck cancer survivor, and mama to children "from hard places." Michele is acutely aware of our deep need for the presence of God, and she shares her search for Him in her most recent book, *Relentless: The Unshakeable Presence of a God Who Never Leaves*. Michele lives in Colorado with her husband and six children. Visit her at michelecushatt .com or on social media @michelecushatt.

Robin Dance is an aging specialist, author, speaker, and life plan advisor whose relatable encouragement and insight daily inspire others in person, in print, and online. Southern as sugar-shocked tea, she's an empty-nesting mom of three married to her college sweetheart and currently living in the heart of Georgia. Learn more at robindance.me or connect on Instagram @robindance.me.

Holley Gerth is the *Wall Street Journal* bestselling author of *The Powerful Purpose of Introverts: Why the World Needs You to Be You*. She imagines a world where we all become who we're created to be, use our strengths to serve, and grow for a lifetime. Connect with Holley at holleygerth.com or on social media @holleygerth.

Dorina Lazo Gilmore-Young is passionate about helping women discover God's glory on life's unexpected paths and flourish in their God-given callings. Dorina is a speaker and podcaster and has published children's books, Bible studies, poetry, and a devotional, *Walk Run Soar*. She and her husband, Shawn, are raising three brave daughters in central

California. Connect with her at DorinaGilmore.com or on Instagram @dorinagilmore.

Bonnie Gray is the author of *Sweet Like Jasmine* and *Whispers of Rest*. As a speaker and podcast host of *BREATHE: The Stress Less Podcast*, Bonnie empowers women toward emotional wellness through soul care and biblical encouragement as God's beloved. She lives in California with her husband and two sons. Visit her on Instagram @thebonnie gray or at thebonniegray.com.

Joy Groblebe is the content marketing director for DaySpring, leading (in)courage behind the scenes. She lives in Oklahoma with her husband, two pit bulls, and four very loud kids. Her life is a grateful mix of family, friends who are family, and travel . . . lots of travel.

Simi John was born in India and raised in Texas. She is married to Jayson, who serves as a lead pastor at their local church, and they have two children. Simi is a speaker and author. Her passion is to empower women to walk confidently in their God-given identity. Connect with her at simijohn.tv or on Instagram @simijohn.

Tasha Jun is a melancholy dreamer, a biracial Korean American storyteller, wife to Matt, and mama to three little warriors. Writing has always been the way God has held her shalom-sick heart together and led her toward hope. Tasha's first book about identity and belonging is due to release in May 2023. Learn more at tashajun.com or on Instagram @tashajunb.

Rachel Marie Kang is a writer of prose, poems, and other pieces. She is the author of *Let There Be Art*, and her writing has been featured in *Christianity Today*, *Charlotte Magazine*, and at (in)courage. Rachel lives and writes from North Carolina at rachelmariekang.com and on Instagram @rachelmariekang.

Aliza Latta is a Canadian artist and author who is a huge fan of telling stories. Her artwork and writing have been featured in publications for LifeWay, DaySpring, and (in)courage. She is always searching for the goodness of God, even when she has to squint to see it. Visit her at alizalatta.com or on Instagram @alizalatta.

Jennifer Dukes Lee is the author of *Growing Slow* and *It's All Under Control*. She and her husband live on the fifth-generation Lee family farm in northwest Iowa, where they are raising crops, pigs, and two beautiful humans. Find her at jenniferdukeslee.com and on social media @jenniferdukeslee.

Kathi Lipp lives with her husband, Roger, and a bunch of chickens in the Sierra Nevada Mountains of California. There they host writer retreats, and Kathi writes about how to do life with God a little closer today than yesterday. She's a bestselling author and absolutely loves her Clutter Free Community on Facebook. Connect with Kathi at kathilipp.com and on Facebook @authorkathilipp.

Jami Nato is wife to Nato and mom to four unruly children. She is an entrepreneur and leader who focuses on faith, community, authenticity, and courage. Jami is passionate about hoarding socks and not doing laundry, and she loves using awkward humor and honesty to convey the truth of the gospel and navigate tough conversations. Find her on Instagram @jaminato.

Anjuli Paschall grew up encircled by an orange grove in San Diego. She earned her master's degree in spiritual formation and soul care from Talbot Seminary. She currently lives in Southern California with her husband (a pastor) and their five children. Anjuli is the author of *Stay* and *Awake*. Chai tea, the ocean, and the color orange are a few of her favorite things. Visit her at anjulipaschall.com or on Instagram @lovealways.anjuli.

Patricia Raybon is an award-winning Colorado author and novelist whose book with her daughter is titled *Undivided: A Muslim Daughter, Her Christian Mother, Their Path to Peace*. She also writes the Annalee Spain Mystery series set in Colorado. Patricia and her husband, Dan, have two grown daughters, five grandchildren, and a granddog named Max. Connect with her at patriciaraybon.com.

Michelle Ami Reyes, PhD, is the vice president of the Asian American Christian Collaborative and co-executive director of Pax. She is the scholar in residence at Hope Community Church and author of *Becoming All Things: How Small Changes Lead to Lasting Connections Across Cultures*. Michelle lives in Austin, Texas, with her husband and two amazing kids. Find her at michelleamireyes.com or on Instagram @michelleamireyes.

Jen Schmidt loves to encourage, challenge, and cheer on women in both the beauty and bedlam of their everyday lives. A popular speaker, host of the Becoming conference, and author of *Just Open the Door*, Jen invites you to the joy of open-door living. Follow her on Instagram @jenschmidt_beauty andbedlam or go to beautyandbedlam.com.

Kristen Strong, author of *When Change Finds You, Back Roads to Belonging*, and *Girl Meets Change*, writes as a friend helping you see a more hopeful view of your difficult life change. She and her US Air Force veteran husband, David, have three children. Connect with Kristen at kristenstrong.com and on Instagram @kristenstrong.

Renee Swope is a Word-lover, heart-encourager, and grace-needer. The bestselling author of *A Confident Heart* and her new release, *A Confident Mom*, Renee is a mom of two grown sons and a tweenage daughter. She loves gardening, making memories with her family, and creating beautiful spaces in her home. Find her at reneeswope.com and on social media @reneeswope.

Melissa Zaldivar is a speaker and researcher living near Boston, Massachusetts, and is the author of *Kingdom Come* (and a second book on the way!). She holds a master's degree in theology and a bachelor's in communications, and you can usually find her browsing in an antique store, leading tours at Orchard House, or walking along the coast. Connect with her at melissazaldivar.com or on Instagram @melissazaldivar.

(in)courage welcomes you

to an online community of women who seek Jesus together. Each weekday we meet you right where you are, as one of our thirty writers shares what's going on in her everyday life, and how God's right in the middle of it all. They bring their unique experiences—joys and struggles equally—so that you can feel less alone and be empowered by the hope Jesus gives. **Learn more and join the sisterhood at incourage.me**.

Join us at **www.incourage.me** and connect with us on social media!

Seeking a heart of hope, peace, wisdom, and mercy? We've got you.

This Bible study collection from (in)courage pairs Scripture with story in a way that will ignite your faith and lead you to the full life in Christ that you long for. Packed with solid observation, interpretation, and application of Scripture, plus daily prayers and weekly memory verses, each study will strengthen your relationship with the Lord.

Join the
SIMPLE DIFFERENCE
Movement

Rather than telling you to do more, *The Simple Difference* shows you how to see more: more of the people in front of you, more of God's lavish love for you, more of His power within you. With this book, you can discover ways to impact those around you, realize your limitations don't need to hold you back, and learn to see the beauty in your community.

---

100 Days of Real-Life Hope

In this 100-day devotional, the (in)courage community reaches into the grief and pain of both crisis and ordinary life. Each day includes a key Scripture, a heartening devotion, and a prayer to remind you that God is near and hope is possible. You won't find tidy bows or trite quick fixes, just arrows pointing you straight to Jesus.

Lightning Source UK Ltd.
Milton Keynes UK
UKHW042137021122
411551UK00002B/11

9 780800 742454